Crypto and Cash Flow:
A Business Owners Guide to Financial Freedom

Christopher O'Neal, CPA, MBA

Copyright © 2024 Christopher O'Neal, CPA, MBA

All rights reserved.

ISBN: 9798302212092

DEDICATION

A Moment of Gratitude

They say it takes a village to raise a child, and I've found the same is true for tackling something as fascinating and complex as cryptocurrency. This book wouldn't exist without the encouragement, insights, and patience of so many along the way.

To my wife and family: thank you for tolerating my late-night crypto revelations, endless YouTube marathons, and dinnertime blockchain lectures. Your love and patience made this possible.

To Shyla, Eric, and Scott—your wisdom, vision, and mentorship opened doors to new business possibilities and helped shape my journey, thank you.

Special thanks to my friend Trevor for introducing me to the crypto universe, and to my brother Brian for keeping me laughing while pushing me to dive deeper.

Finally, to the global crypto community—builders, dreamers, skeptics—you are the reason this digital revolution thrives. Thank you for inspiring me to explore and contribute.

This book is as much yours as it is mine. Let's keep shaping the future, one block at a time.

Forward

Welcome to the New Frontier

In a world where financial landscapes are evolving faster than the latest TikTok trend, it's time for business owners to ditch outdated strategies and embrace the bold new frontier of crypto and cash flow. Let's face it—no one dreams of crunching spreadsheets when they could be planning their moonshot investments or simply making payroll without breaking a sweat. This book is your roadmap to navigating these uncharted waters with clarity, humor, and just enough geekiness to impress your friends.

Whether you're here because you've heard buzzwords like "blockchain" and "NFT" or because cash flow management feels like trying to tame a wild horse, you've come to the right place. We'll demystify cryptocurrency, master the art of liquidity, and, most importantly, keep your financial future from looking like a game of roulette.

So grab your favorite beverage (yes, coffee counts as a financial planning tool), and let's dive into the adventure ahead. Welcome to the future of finance—it's going to be a ride.

This book serves as an indispensable guide for those seeking to not only survive but thrive in this dynamic environment. If you're reading this, you're already ahead of the curve, and this book is your ticket to staying there. If you've read my previous book, **Cash Flow**

Cure, you'll recognize some of the foundational strategies for cash flow management here. But in this book, we take those principles further, applying them to the dynamic world of cryptocurrency and blockchain.

Within the pages of this book, readers will embark on a comprehensive journey through the intricate world of cryptocurrency and the often-misunderstood realm of cash flow. It's a journey that transcends the technical jargon and theoretical complexities, offering instead a practical, accessible, and even humorous exploration of these critical aspects of modern business.

The book is divided into three parts:

Part 1: Crypto delves into the fascinating world of cryptocurrency, unraveling the mysteries of blockchain technology and its potential to revolutionize finance. Readers will gain a foundational understanding of Bitcoin, the pioneer of cryptocurrencies, and its unique characteristics as a decentralized digital asset. The book goes beyond Bitcoin, exploring the diverse landscape of altcoins, from Ethereum with its smart contract capabilities to the meme-coin phenomenon of Shiba Inu, highlighting the importance of diversification and risk management in this volatile market.

Part 2: Cash Flow shifts the focus to the often-overlooked but essential aspect of cash flow management. Readers will discover the critical distinction between profit and cash flow, recognizing that a healthy bottom line doesn't always translate to a healthy bank balance. The book provides practical strategies for optimizing cash flow, from mastering the art of receivables collection and expense management to securing short-term financing and navigating seasonal fluctuations. Readers will learn how to identify and avoid common cash flow pitfalls, ensuring their businesses have the financial resilience to weather any storm.

Part 3: Financial Freedom connects the dots between cryptocurrency, cash flow management, and the ultimate goal of financial independence. Readers will explore the true meaning of financial freedom, recognizing that it's not just about accumulating wealth but about having the choice, flexibility, and security to live a life aligned with their values and aspirations. The book provides a step-by-step guide to creating a financial freedom roadmap, setting ambitious goals, and developing a freedom-based mindset that empowers readers to take control of their financial future. This book is more than just a guide; it's a conversation, a journey with a trusted advisor who understands the challenges and opportunities that business owners face in today's ever-changing world. It's filled with real-world examples, actionable strategies, and a healthy dose of humor, making the learning process not only informative but also enjoyable.

Whether you're a seasoned entrepreneur or just starting your business journey, this book will equip you with the knowledge, tools, and inspiration you need to navigate the exciting world of crypto and cash flow management. It's a book that will challenge your assumptions, expand your horizons, and empower you to build a business that supports your dreams and fuels your financial freedom.

So, dive in, explore the possibilities, and let this book be your guide to unlocking a future where your financial aspirations become reality.

Oh, yeah....the typoes are on the house. You're welcome!

Enjoy!

CONTENTS

Disclaimer i

Part 1: Crypto

1. Cryptocurrency 101: Why It's Not Just for Tech Nerds Anymore ... 1
2. Blockchain: The Digital Ledger, You Didn't Know You Needed ... 11
3. Crypto Volatility: HODLing on for Dear Life ... 20
4. Accepting Crypto as Payment ... 29
5. Decentralized Finance (DeFi): The New Frontier of Business Funding ... 36
6. NFTs and the Metaverse: Building Brands in the Digital Frontier ... 43
7. Beyond Bitcoin: The Altcoin Explosion ... 47

Part 2: Cash Flow

8. Profit's a Liar – Why Cash Flow Is the Real King ... 59
9. Cash Flow Strategies for the Modern Business: Show Me the Money! ... 68
10. Avoiding Cash Flow Crunches: How to Stay Liquid in a Digital World ... 77
11. From Red to Black: Getting Your Cash Flow in the Positive ... 85

Part 3: Financial Freedom

12	Financial Freedom: More Than Just a Buzzword	92
13	Creating a Financial Freedom Roadmap: Destination Independence	101

Bonus Materials

14	Advanced Crypto Strategies	113
15	Expanding Horizons: Global and Sustainable Trends	119
16	Future-Proofing Your Business: Legal and Compliance Essentials	123
	Glossary	130
	References	134
	Tools	135
	Appendix A: Satoshi Kakamoto's White Paper	138
	Appendix B: Example Financial Freedom Roadmap	148
	About the Author (That One Guy)	153

Disclaimer

The Limits of Advice: A Light-Hearted Note on Risk

This book is intended for educational purposes only. It's not intended to provide specific financial, investment, or accounting advice, so please don't blame us if you invest in a meme coin based on the alignment of Jupiter and your pet goldfish. *While the author is a Certified Public Accountant (CPA), he is not your CPA (unless you hire him, in which case, he is).* The information provided should not be considered a substitute for professional advice from a qualified financial advisor, accountant, or other professional. The author and publisher do not guarantee the accuracy or completeness of the information provided and are not responsible for any losses or damages that may result from its use.

Part 1: Crypto

Introducing readers to the world of cryptocurrency, covering essentials, tech basics, and strategies for navigating the crypto landscape.

Chapter 1: "Cryptocurrency 101: Why It's Not Just for Tech Nerds Anymore"

A beginner's guide to crypto with humor to ease the learning curve.

Overview of Cryptocurrency Basics

What Is Cryptocurrency?

Cryptocurrency is like the cool kid at the financial playground—it's digital money but with a rebellious streak. Imagine cash that never crumples, coins that never jingle, and payments that can zip across the globe in seconds. That's crypto.

Crypto is Venmo's cooler, independent cousin—speedy, private, and far less interested in snooping through your transaction history. Think James Bond, but for money. Or like your coffee shop loyalty points—except these can buy way more than a latte (and won't expire if you ignore them). Crypto offers speed, security, and global accessibility, making it a game-changer for anyone with an internet connection.

Key Takeaway: Cryptocurrency is digital money that's fast, secure, and borderless.

A Brief History of Cryptocurrency: From Niche to Mainstream

Cryptocurrency's origin story reads like a modern-day tech thriller. It all began in October 31, 2008 when an anonymous figure—or possibly a group—known as Satoshi Nakamoto released a nine-page white paper titled *Bitcoin: A Peer-to-Peer Electronic Cash System*. Think of it as the "Declaration of Independence" for digital money. In it, Nakamoto outlined a revolutionary vision: a decentralized currency free from banks, intermediaries, and government control. If most financial white papers are as dry as a legal contract, Nakamoto's is a masterpiece of clarity and innovation. (Want to explore the whole thing? **Check out Appendix A!**)

Building on that vision, Nakamoto introduced Bitcoin to the world in 2009—a decentralized, peer-to-peer digital currency with the promise of financial freedom. Think of Bitcoin as the indie garage band that nobody noticed until it started topping charts globally.

By 2010, Bitcoin was gaining traction, with its first real-world transaction—a purchase of two pizzas for 10,000 BTC (now worth millions). The crypto world expanded in 2015 with the launch of Ethereum, which brought smart contracts and decentralized applications (DApps) into the spotlight, setting the stage for crypto to be more than just digital money.

The years that followed saw an explosion of altcoins like Litecoin and Ripple, as well as quirky meme coins such as Dogecoin, proving that crypto could be both innovative and playful. By 2020, cryptocurrency had reached mainstream recognition, with institutional investors and major companies like Tesla and PayPal joining the bandwagon.

Key Takeaway: Cryptocurrency has evolved from a niche experiment into a global financial revolution, offering opportunities that were unimaginable just a decade ago.

What Does "Decentralized" Mean?

Decentralization is what makes crypto stand out in the financial world. Instead of banks or governments running the show, it's powered by a network of computers worldwide. Picture a giant digital notebook where every transaction is recorded and verified by thousands of users. No one can erase or alter the record without everyone else agreeing—goodbye, fraud!

Real-World Analogy:
Imagine organizing a group potluck where everyone keeps track of what food is coming. If someone tries to bring two bags of chips and calls it a gourmet meal, the group vetoes it. That's decentralization—group accountability without a bossy host.

Key Takeaway: Decentralization removes central authority, replacing it with a transparent and collaborative system.

How Does It Work?

Crypto runs on something called blockchain—a public digital ledger. When you make a transaction, it's like adding a new chapter to a never-ending book. Everyone on the network gets a copy, ensuring that no one can mess with the story.

Real-World Example:

Think of PayPal or Venmo, but instead of one company managing the transactions, the entire system runs on a global network. No one person or company owns it, which means no single point of failure.

Key Takeaway: Crypto uses blockchain to securely record and verify transactions across a decentralized network.

Mining: The Digital Gold Rush

Imagine being part of a global treasure hunt, but instead of shovels and pickaxes, you're armed with computers and code. This is cryptocurrency mining in a nutshell. Miners are the unsung heroes of the crypto world, verifying transactions and securing the blockchain by solving complex mathematical puzzles.

Here's how it works: When a transaction occurs, miners compete to solve a cryptographic puzzle. The winner adds the transaction to a new "block" on the blockchain and is rewarded with newly minted cryptocurrency. This process ensures that every transaction is verified, making it nearly impossible to manipulate the system.

However, mining isn't all fun and games. It's resource-intensive, often requiring powerful computers and substantial energy. To address environmental concerns, many miners are turning to renewable energy sources, making the process more sustainable.

Real-World Example:

In Iceland, crypto miners tap into the country's abundant geothermal energy to power their operations, proving that mining can be both efficient and green.

Cross Mining keeps the crypto ecosystem alive and secure, but its energy demands have sparked innovation and debate about sustainability.

Blockchain: The Backbone of Cryptocurrency

Picture a magical notebook shared among thousands of friends. Whenever someone writes in it, everyone's copy is instantly updated. If someone tries to change their entry, everyone else's copy rejects the alteration. This is how blockchain works—an unalterable, transparent, and decentralized digital ledger.

In technical terms, blockchain records transactions in "blocks" that are linked together in chronological order. Each block is verified by a network of computers (or nodes), ensuring accuracy and security.

Why does this matter?

Blockchain removes the need for intermediaries such as banks or payment processors, enabling transactions to be quicker, more cost-effective, and highly secure.

Real-World Example:

Walmart uses blockchain to trace the origins of food products. In case of contamination, the company can identify the source within seconds, saving time, money, and lives.

Key Takeaway: Blockchain isn't just the engine behind cryptocurrency; it's a revolutionary technology with the potential to transform industries from finance to healthcare.

Why Use Cryptocurrency?

1. **Speed:** Cross-border bank transfers can take days; crypto takes minutes.
   Example: A freelancer in Argentina can receive payment from a U.S. client in under an hour using Bitcoin—faster than any wire transfer. It's like choosing a private jet over a mule-drawn cart—the difference isn't just speed; it's about convenience and sophistication.
2. **Lower Fees:** Forget the 3% fee your credit card charges. Crypto transactions often cost just pennies.
   Example: Overstock saved thousands in processing fees by accepting Bitcoin instead of traditional payment methods.
3. **Global Access:** 1.4 billion people don't have access to banks but do have smartphones. Crypto is their ticket to the financial system.
4. **Privacy and Security:** Your transactions aren't tied to your identity. Plus, no single hacker can compromise the network.

Example: In countries with strict financial controls, crypto has allowed citizens to bypass restrictions and access their funds securely.

"What's in Your Digital Wallet?"

Think of your crypto wallet as the ultimate digital fanny pack (without the stigma of wearing one)—it's secure, lightweight, and holds all your essentials. But unlike your regular wallet, it won't have a crumpled receipt from your last coffee run.

Here's the deal: crypto wallets come in two types—**hot** and **cold**. Hot wallets are like your regular debit card, connected to the internet for easy access. Cold wallets? They're the high-security vaults, like burying gold in your backyard (but much cooler, literally).

Hot Wallet Example:

You've got Bitcoin on an app like Coinbase. It's accessible for trading but more prone to cyber pickpockets.

Cold Wallet Example:

A hardware wallet, like Ledger Nano, is disconnected from the web, making it hacker-proof. It's the Fort Knox of crypto storage—if Fort Knox could fit in your pocket.

While it might be tempting to leave your cryptocurrency on an exchange (it's convenient, right?), doing so is like storing all your valuables at a mall kiosk instead of a bank vault. Exchanges are prime targets for hackers, and history is full of stories where unsuspecting users lost their funds overnight. By transferring your crypto to a private wallet, you take control of your assets—no third-party middleman who can lose, mismanage, or lock you out.

Example: Take the infamous Mt. Gox exchange hack of 2014, where 850,000 Bitcoin disappeared into the ether—worth billions today. Thousands of users lost their savings because they trusted the exchange to keep their crypto safe. On the other hand, wallets like

Ledger or Trezor act like Fort Knox for your digital gold, keeping hackers at bay as long as you safeguard your private key.

Key Takeaway: Choose your wallet wisely. For frequent traders, hot wallets offer convenience. For HODLers, cold wallets are your best bet. And no matter what, never store your passwords on a sticky note.

Humorous Take: If banks make you feel like a goldfish in a tank, crypto turns you into a dolphin—free to swim wherever you want.

Key Takeaway: Crypto is fast, cheap, and inclusive—a financial tool for the modern, globalized world.

What Is an Asset Class? Why Bitcoin Fits the Definition

An asset class is a category of investments, like cash, stocks, or real estate. Bitcoin has carved out its own niche as an "alternative asset," offering unique benefits like scarcity and investment potential.

Why Bitcoin Is Like Digital Gold

1. **Scarcity:** Bitcoin's supply is capped at 21 million coins—no inflation here.
   Example: Gold has value because it's rare. Bitcoin takes this idea to the digital realm.
2. **Store of Value:** Bitcoin is seen as a hedge against inflation, much like gold.
   Example: During the pandemic, Bitcoin surged as investors sought alternatives to traditional assets.
3. **Investment Potential:** Many hold Bitcoin as an investment, hoping its value will rise over time.
   Example: MicroStrategy turned heads when it made Bitcoin a core part of its corporate treasury, reaping significant gains.

Key Takeaway: Bitcoin isn't just currency—it's an investment asset with a growing place in the financial ecosystem.

Why Now? The Case for Crypto in Business

Businesses That Have Embraced Crypto

1. **Tesla:** Invested $1.5 billion in Bitcoin and briefly accepted it for car payments.
2. **Starbucks:** Allows customers to pay with Bitcoin through the Bakkt app.
3. **Overstock:** Early adopter of crypto payments, cutting transaction fees and attracting tech-savvy customers.

Lower Transaction Costs

Traditional payment methods charge hefty fees. Crypto eliminates middlemen, saving businesses money.

Example: A Miami coffee shop reduced costs by 2% per transaction by accepting Ethereum for payments, appealing to the city's crypto-friendly clientele.

Risks and Rewards: High-Level Considerations

The Rewards

1. **Global Reach:** Crypto opens new markets, especially in underbanked regions.
2. **Lower Costs:** Save money on transaction fees compared to traditional methods.
3. **High Returns:** The potential for price appreciation makes Bitcoin an attractive investment.

The Risks

1. **Volatility:** Prices can swing wildly, creating challenges for businesses accepting crypto.
   Example: Tesla halted Bitcoin payments after its value fluctuated too much.
2. **Regulation:** Governments are still figuring out how to handle crypto.
   Example: China's crackdown on crypto caused a market-wide dip in 2021.
3. **Security:** Losing your private key means losing access to your funds.
   Example: The infamous Mt. Gox hack in 2014 remains a cautionary tale.

Key Takeaway: Crypto's rewards are exciting, but the risks require careful planning and management.

Where to Go When Crypto Jargon Makes Your Brain Hurt

Learning about cryptocurrency can feel like trying to decode an alien language—with the aliens actively laughing at you. But don't worry, even the pros started somewhere. Here are some beginner-friendly resources to make sense of it all (and maybe even impress your friends at the next dinner party):

- **CoinDesk:** Think of CoinDesk as the New York Times of the crypto world—except their headlines are less about politics and more about how Bitcoin is *maybe* going to the moon (or crashing). They have everything from beginner guides to deep dives on DeFi and NFTs. Warning: You might leave smarter, but your browser history will look like you're training to be a crypto guru.
- **Decrypt:** If CoinDesk is the NYT, Decrypt is BuzzFeed with a degree in blockchain. Their writing is fun, approachable, and won't make your brain ache. Plus, they've got a podcast—so you can sound informed without actually reading. Perfect for multitaskers.

- **The Block:** This one's for when you're feeling ambitious (or pretending to be). Their research reports and analyses are top-notch, but you might need a second cup of coffee to get through some of the heavier stuff.

Chapter Wrap-Up: Why You Should Care About Crypto

Crypto isn't just for tech nerds anymore. It's a tool for financial freedom, offering speed, inclusivity, and investment potential. Whether you're a business owner looking to cut costs or an investor seeking the next big thing, crypto has something to offer. The key is to dive in with a clear head, an informed plan, and a willingness to adapt.

However, before you dive headfirst into the next chapter, here's a challenge specifically for you. After all, understanding crypto isn't just about reading—it's about rolling up your sleeves and taking action. Think of this as your first step into the digital frontier, with no pressure and plenty of room for curiosity.

7-Day Crypto Challenge:

- Day 1: Set up a crypto wallet.
- Day 2: Research 3 cryptocurrencies and their use cases.
- Day 3: Buy $10 worth of Bitcoin.
- Day 4: Track Bitcoin's price movements over 24 hours.
- Day 5: Learn about one altcoin.
- Day 6: Explore a crypto payment gateway (e.g., Coinbase Commerce).
- Day 7: Reflect on what you've learned and decide your next steps.

Chapter 2: Blockchain: The Digital Ledger, You Didn't Know You Needed

Breaking down blockchain without the techie jargon—think of it as the accounting of the future.

What if I told you the technology behind cryptocurrency could also transform industries like healthcare, real estate, and even your morning coffee? Blockchain isn't just a buzzword—it's a revolution in trust and transparency, one digital ledger at a time.

To understand its impact, think of blockchain as the Swiss Army knife of technology. It's versatile, secure, and surprisingly easy to understand once you strip away the jargon. By the end of this chapter, you'll see why world leaders, tech giants, and even coffee chains are embracing this game-changing innovation.

Blockchain might sound like something cooked up in a sci-fi writer's lab, but at its core, it's a straightforward concept. Think of it as the ledger that accountants, business owners, and even nosy neighbors have always dreamed of: one that's secure, transparent, and completely tamper-proof. Whether you're managing a Fortune 500 company or just trying to keep track of your kids' allowance payments, blockchain is here to level up your record-keeping game.

Blockchain Demystified

What Exactly Is Blockchain?

Imagine a magical notebook. Each time someone writes in it, an identical copy of that page appears in thousands of notebooks all over the world. If someone tries to change their page—like scribbling out "$50 paid" and replacing it with "$500 paid"—the rest of the notebooks instantly catch the fraud. That's blockchain in a nutshell.

Blockchain is a digital ledger where every transaction is permanently recorded. It's decentralized, meaning it's not stored in one location but across a network of computers. This makes it secure and tamper-resistant—no sneaky pencil erasers allowed.

Think of it as the neighborhood gossip chain, except this one doesn't embellish stories—it sticks to the facts, and everyone gets the same, verified update.

The MIT Sloan article 'Blockchain, explained' emphasizes the potential of blockchain to reduce two key costs for businesses: the cost of verification and the cost of networking, thus transforming digital platforms and how businesses operate.

Key Takeaway: Blockchain is a shared, digital ledger that's decentralized, transparent, and virtually unalterable. Keep in mind, Blockchain isn't just a buzzword; it ensures transparency, security, and efficiency in transactions. It powers cryptocurrency, but its potential extends to healthcare, supply chains, and even voting systems. Understanding it gives you a competitive edge in the digital economy.

Real-World Analogy: The Neighborhood Ledger

Imagine your neighborhood starts a communal garden fund, and everyone keeps a notebook tracking the funds. One neighbor tries to sneak in a $500 'rose bush expense' that's really for their weekend getaway—guess what? Everyone else's notebooks call foul. Blockchain works the same way but on a massive, digital scale—with no room for mistakes, fraud, or "creative math."

In their research on the Bitcoin market, Schoar and Makarov found that blockchain technology can significantly reduce the cost of verifying transactions, eliminating the need for traditional intermediaries like banks.

A Quick History of Blockchain (Without the Jargon)

Blockchain burst onto the scene in 2009 with Bitcoin, thanks to an anonymous creator named Satoshi Nakamoto. Think of Nakamoto as the Willy Wonka of crypto, gifting the world a revolutionary way to exchange value without middlemen like banks. Since then, blockchain has grown far beyond Bitcoin, influencing industries like healthcare, real estate, and supply chains.

Blockchain vs. Traditional Ledgers

The Traditional Ledger: Old Reliable

Traditional ledgers—whether digital or on paper—are centralized, meaning one party controls the records. Banks, companies, and governments maintain these ledgers, relying on layers of checks and balances. While this system has worked for centuries, it's far from perfect. It's prone to human error, inefficiency, and occasionally, fraud.

Blockchain's "Turbocharged" Upgrade

With blockchain, ledgers are decentralized and stored across thousands of computers. Transactions are recorded in real-time, verified by the network, and permanently locked in. No more waiting days for a bank to process a transfer or digging through piles of receipts during an audit.

Real-World Example: Walmart's Blockchain for Food Safety
Walmart uses blockchain to track its supply chain, allowing the company to trace food origins in seconds instead of days.

Key Takeaway: Blockchain eliminates middlemen, speeds up processes, and ensures transparency—like a turbocharged CPA who never needs coffee breaks.

As Catalini explains in 'Blockchain, explained,' the technology offers a cost-effective way to verify transactions, allowing for secure transactions without revealing the underlying information to third parties.

Furthermore, Catalini highlights that blockchain technology can reduce the cost of building and running a network, enabling decentralized platforms without central control, thus increasing competition and creating opportunities for new business models.

Schoar and Makarov's research supports the idea that blockchain technology has the potential to revolutionize sectors beyond finance, particularly those dealing with digital assets and requiring secure, transparent transactions.

Blockchain for Audits: The Future of Financial Transparency

Imagine audits where you don't have to dig through boxes of receipts. Blockchain stores every transaction in an unalterable, chronological order, making verification a breeze. Instead of hunting for evidence, auditors can scan the blockchain and confirm everything instantly.

Real-World Example: Walmart

When Walmart used blockchain to trace contaminated lettuce, they identified the source in seconds instead of days, saving millions in potential recalls. Imagine how this transparency could transform your supply chain!

Blockchain and Healthcare: A Cure for Data Headaches

In healthcare, blockchain secures patient records and ensures accuracy. Imagine visiting a new doctor and having your medical history instantly available—with your permission. No paperwork, no errors, no waiting weeks for records to transfer.

Blockchain for Medical Records

In **healthcare**, blockchain has the potential to eliminate one of the most frustrating bottlenecks: medical record management. Estonia's healthcare system leads the way, using blockchain to securely store and share patient data. This ensures that records are accurate, accessible, and tamper-proof, empowering patients and streamlining provider workflows. Imagine a system where your medical history is a few clicks away, but only when you allow access—a far cry from the current chaos of paper forms and misplaced records.

Blockchain in Real Estate: Cutting Through the Clutter

Real estate deals are notorious for paperwork and delays. Blockchain streamlines the process by storing contracts and ownership records securely.

Real-World Example: Propy's Blockchain Platform

Propy uses blockchain to simplify real estate transactions. They've facilitated deals in California and beyond, cutting the closing process from weeks to hours. Say goodbye to piles of documents and hello to fast, transparent deals.

Credential Verification with Blockchain

Education is another sector where blockchain is making waves, particularly in credential verification. MIT's Digital Diploma initiative provides graduates with tamper-proof, blockchain-secured diplomas that employers can instantly verify. This innovation not only saves time and reduces fraud but also ensures that students maintain control over their academic records—a game-changer for a world where credentials are increasingly vital.

Blockchain in Supply Chains: Following the Journey

Blockchain tracks products from origin to destination, making supply chains more transparent and efficient.

Real-World Example: De Beers and Diamonds

De Beers uses blockchain to track diamonds, ensuring they're ethically sourced and conflict-free. Buyers can trace their diamond's journey from the mine to the jewelry store, boosting transparency and trust.

Key Takeaway: Blockchain is transforming industries by enhancing transparency, security, and efficiency—from healthcare to real estate and beyond.

Blockchain for Supply Chain Transparency

In **agriculture**, blockchain technology is transforming supply chains. A coffee cooperative in Colombia uses blockchain to track its beans from farm to cup, ensuring fair trade compliance and quality. Consumers can scan a QR code on their coffee bag to trace the journey of their purchase, from the farmer who grew the beans to the roaster who perfected the flavor. This transparency builds trust and strengthens consumer loyalty.

Blockchain: Coming Soon to a Coffee Shop Near You"

You might think blockchain is all about Bitcoin and boring financial ledgers, but its potential is as broad as your Netflix recommendations.

Imagine this:

- **Coffee Loyalty Programs:** Instead of paper punch cards, blockchain tracks your free latte in a tamper-proof system. No more "accidentally" adding extra punches!
- **Music Royalties:** Artists get paid instantly when their songs are streamed—no middlemen taking a cut.
- **Election Security:** Blockchain could ensure votes are tamper-proof. (Finally, a tech solution we can all agree on!)

Key Takeaway: Blockchain's future isn't just about crypto—it's about improving the everyday systems we rely on. Whether it's your morning coffee or your next vote, blockchain might just be running the show.

Cryptocurrency in Business: From Payments to Payroll

Businesses are increasingly leveraging cryptocurrency to innovate and save money. Here's how:

1. **Accepting Crypto Payments**: Many companies now accept Bitcoin, Ethereum, and other cryptocurrencies for goods and services. For example:
    - **Starbucks** allows customers to use Bitcoin through the Bakkt app, catering to tech-savvy coffee lovers.
    - **Overstock** was one of the first major retailers to accept Bitcoin, reducing transaction fees and attracting a crypto-savvy audience.

2. **Paying Employees in Crypto**: Forward-thinking companies like **Coinbase** and **Bitwage** let employees choose cryptocurrency for part (or all) of their paycheck. This approach is popular in the tech sector and among remote workers in countries with unstable local currencies.
3. **Cross-Border Transactions**: Crytocurrency steamlines global payments by removing intermediaries, cutting fees, and significantly reducing processing times.
    - *Example*: A U.S.-based freelance platform uses stablecoins like USDC to pay contractors in developing countries, bypassing high conversion fees and delays.
4. **Fundraising Through Crypto**: Companies like **Tesla** have explored crypto for corporate treasury strategies, using Bitcoin as a hedge against inflation.

Key Takeaway: From reducing transaction fees to accessing new markets, cryptocurrency is reshaping the way businesses operate.

Crypto Wallets: Choosing the Right One

If blockchain is the engine behind cryptocurrency, wallets are the keys that let you drive. A crypto wallet is where you store your digital assets securely—and picking the right one is crucial. Here's a quick breakdown:
- **Hot Wallets**: These are connected to the internet and are ideal for frequent transactions. Examples include apps like Coinbase or MetaMask. While convenient, they're more vulnerable to hacking.
    - *Use Case*: Daily trading or quick payments.
- **Cold Wallets**: Offline wallets, like hardware devices or even paper, offer unparalleled security. My personal favorite is the **Trezor wallet**—a compact device that keeps my assets safe from digital threats.
    - *Use Case*: Long-term storage or "HODLing" large amounts of cryptocurrency.

Real-World Analogy: Think of a hot wallet as your checking account—easily accessible but less secure. A cold wallet? That's your safe deposit box, tucked away and guarded.

Key Takeaway: For frequent traders, hot wallets are convenient. For long-term security, nothing beats a cold wallet like Trezor.

Chapter Wrap-Up

Blockchain isn't just a buzzword; it's the next evolution in record-keeping. Whether it's ensuring food safety, streamlining real estate deals, or securing medical records, blockchain is reshaping how industries operate.

If you're a business owner, don't wait for blockchain to become the norm. Start exploring how this technology can enhance transparency, reduce costs, and future-proof your operations.

Ready to dig deeper? In the next chapter, we'll explore how blockchain and cryptocurrency are intertwined and how businesses can leverage this partnership to thrive in a digital-first world. Buckle up—your crash course in crypto's potential is just getting started.

Chapter 3: Crypto Volatility: HODLing on for Dear Life

How to handle crypto's wild roller-coaster ride while keeping your sanity intact.

Cryptocurrency is like the teenager of the financial world: unpredictable, high-energy, and full of potential, but prone to dramatic outbursts. While some investors thrive on the thrill, others find themselves clutching their metaphorical seatbelts, asking, "Why did I sign up for this?"

This chapter is your survival guide for the ups, downs, and loop-de-loops of crypto volatility. Whether you're in it for the moonshots or just trying to avoid a financial nosedive, we'll explore how to navigate the chaos with a cool head—and maybe even a smile.

Understanding Volatility

Why Is Crypto So Volatile?

If the stock market is like a calm cruise ship, cryptocurrency is a jet ski with a hyperactive driver. Its erratic behavior comes down to a few key factors:

1. **Market Maturity:** Crypto is still the new kid on the block. Compared to stocks, which have centuries of data and stability, Bitcoin isn't even old enough to rent a car. Young markets are like toddlers—prone to mood swings and tantrums.
2. **Speculation and Hype:** Crypto thrives on excitement, and the internet loves a spectacle. One tweet from Elon Musk, a Reddit rally, or a viral meme, and prices can skyrocket—or plummet—faster than you can refresh your app.
    - **Example:** Remember when Musk tweeted about Dogecoin being "the people's crypto"? The price soared, only to tumble back down after his "Saturday Night Live" appearance. It was a financial soap opera in real-time.
3. **Lack of Regulation:** Without the oversight that traditional markets have, crypto is a bit like the Wild West—full of opportunity but not without risks.

Key Takeaway: Crypto's volatility stems from its youth, hype-fueled nature, and lack of regulation. Understanding these quirks helps you prepare for the ride.

Market Capitalization: The Size of the Crypto Pond

Market capitalization, or "market cap," is a key metric for evaluating a cryptocurrency's size and relative importance. It's calculated by multiplying the total supply of a cryptocurrency by its current price. For example, Bitcoin, with its limited supply of 21 million coins, commands the highest market cap, making it the "blue chip" of cryptocurrencies.

Why does this matter? Market cap helps you understand a coin's stability and growth potential:

- **Large-Cap Cryptos** (e.g., Bitcoin, Ethereum): Generally more stable, with widespread adoption.

- **Mid-Cap Cryptos**: Offer growth potential but carry higher risks.
- **Small-Cap Cryptos**: High-risk, high-reward options that can either skyrocket or disappear.

Key Takeaway: Market cap is the cryptocurrency world's equivalent of a company's valuation—it reveals the relative size and potential stability of an asset.

How Volatility Impacts Investors

For some, crypto's roller coaster is a chance for big thrills and potential gains. For others, it's a surefire way to develop ulcers. Whether you're a HODLer or a trader, volatility can be both an opportunity and a challenge.

- **HODLers:** Long-term investors who embrace the chaos, trusting that patience will pay off.
- **Traders:** Short-term players who live for the swings, aiming to buy low and sell high.

Key Takeaway: Volatility can be your friend—or your frenemy. Your experience depends on your strategy and tolerance for risk.

The Risks and Challenges of Crypto Investing

While cryptocurrency offers exciting opportunities, it's not without its risks. Here's what you need to watch out for:

1. **Volatility**: Prices can swing dramatically, wiping out gains in hours.
   - *Example*: Bitcoin's price dropped nearly 50% in 2021 within weeks due to market speculation and regulatory news.

2. **Regulatory Uncertainty**: Governments worldwide are still debating how to regulate cryptocurrencies.
    - *Example*: China's crackdown on crypto mining caused a temporary market-wide dip.
3. **Security Risks**: Hackers target exchanges and wallets. A single breach could mean losing your entire investment.
    - *Tip*: Use cold wallets like Trezor to mitigate these risks.
4. **Scams and Fraud**: Rug pulls and Ponzi schemes are common in the crypto space. Be cautious of coins promising "guaranteed returns."
5. **Emotional Investing**: FOMO (Fear of Missing Out) and panic selling can derail your strategy. Stick to your plan.

Key Takeaway: Educating yourself on the risks ensures you enter the crypto market with clear eyes and realistic expectations.

Survival Tactics for the Market Swings

HODLing vs. Trading: Choosing Your Adventure

1. **HODLing:**
    - **The Marathon Mindset:** HODLers believe in crypto's long-term potential. They ride out the dips and focus on the big picture.
    - **Example:** If you bought Bitcoin in 2011 and ignored the noise, you'd be sitting on a fortune today. That's the power of HODLing.
2. **Trading:**
    - **The Sprint Approach:** Traders aim to capitalize on short-term price changes. It's exciting but requires skill, strategy, and nerves of steel.
    - **Example:** Day traders in 2021 made (and lost) fortunes betting on the wild swings of coins like Ethereum and Solana.

Tips for Staying Sane

- **For HODLers:**
    1. **Zoom Out:** Check the yearly trend, not the daily drama.
    2. **Set It and Forget It:** Treat your crypto like a retirement account—buy, hold, and relax.
    3. **Remember Your Why:** If you believe in blockchain's future, it's easier to weather the storms.
- **For Traders:**
    1. **Have a Plan:** Set entry and exit points to avoid emotional decisions.
    2. **Risk What You Can Lose:** Only trade money you're comfortable parting with.
    3. **Stay Cool:** A single tweet shouldn't dictate your financial strategy.

Key Takeaway: Whether you're HODLing or trading, success depends on a clear plan and a steady mindset.

Trusted Voices in Crypto: YouTubers Worth Following

Staying informed in the fast-moving crypto market is crucial. Here are some YouTubers I personally follow for insights:

1. **Austin Hilton**: Known for his approachable style, Austin covers the latest news and trends, especially in meme coins and emerging tokens.
2. **Raoul Pal**: A macroeconomic expert and founder of Real Vision, Raoul dives deep into crypto's intersection with global finance.
3. **Michael Saylor**: The CEO of MicroStrategy and a Bitcoin advocate, Michael offers a corporate perspective on long-term Bitcoin investment strategies.

Key Takeaway: Following reputable influencers can provide valuable insights, but always combine their advice with your research.

Choosing the Right Altcoins: A Practical Guide

With thousands of altcoins available, picking the right ones can feel overwhelming. Here's a framework to simplify your decisions:

1. **Start with Purpose**: Look for coins that solve real-world problems.
    - *Example*: Ethereum powers smart contracts and decentralized apps.
    - *Tip*: Avoid coins that exist purely as hype vehicles.
2. **Check the Team**: A strong development team and transparent leadership are vital.
    - *Red Flag*: Anonymous teams with no track record.
3. **Review the Whitepaper**: This document explains the coin's goals, technology, and roadmap. A lackluster whitepaper is a warning sign.
4. **Evaluate Market Cap and Liquidity**: Opt for coins with enough trading volume to avoid being stuck in an illiquid position.
5. **Use Case Alignment**: Choose coins that align with your investment strategy.
    - *Example*: Long-term HODLers might favor stable platforms like Cardano, while traders could target high-volatility coins like Solana.

Risk Management: Protecting Your Investments

Diversification: The Golden Rule

Avoid putting all your "crypto eggs" in one basket. Diversify your investments across multiple coins to minimize risk and enhance stability.

- **Example:** Pair Bitcoin (the blue chip) with Ethereum (the innovator) and a few smaller coins for growth potential.

Stop-Losses: Your Financial Safety Net

A stop-loss order automatically sells your crypto if prices drop below a certain level. Think of it as a parachute for your portfolio.

- **Tip:** Place stop-losses far enough from your purchase price to avoid selling during normal fluctuations.

Stablecoins: The Crypto Life Raft

Stablecoins, like Tether (USDT) or USD Coin (USDC), are tied to assets like the U.S. dollar. When the market gets turbulent, shifting funds to stablecoins can protect your portfolio while keeping you in the crypto ecosystem.

- **Example:** During a downturn, many investors shift to stablecoins to avoid losses and re-enter when the market stabilizes.

The 80/20 Rule: Balancing Risk

Dedicate 80% of your portfolio to long-term, stable investments and 20% to high-risk, high-reward plays.

- **Example:** Hold Bitcoin and Ethereum as your "steady ships," while allocating a smaller portion to speculative assets like Shiba Inu, Doge or other top 20 meme coins.

Key Takeaway: Risk management isn't about avoiding volatility—it's about preparing for it. Diversify, use tools like stop-losses, and keep your emotions in check.

Interactive Crypto Learning for When You're Too Stressed to HODL

Feeling overwhelmed? Dive into these interactive and community-based resources to get your crypto fix without staring at volatile price charts all day:

- **Khan Academy:** If "free" is your favorite price and you enjoy being talked to like a human, Khan Academy is the answer. Their courses on Bitcoin and blockchain are straightforward and easy to follow—kind of like that one teacher you actually liked in high school.
- **Reddit:** Subreddits like r/CryptoCurrency are where the cool kids (and some trolls) hang out to talk crypto. You'll find FAQs, memes, and debates—but remember, *"Buy Shiba Inu now!"* is not financial advice, no matter how many emojis they use.

Chapter Wrap-Up

Congratulations—you've survived Crypto Volatility 101! Now you know why prices bounce around like a ping-pong ball and how to keep your sanity intact.

Volatility is the spice of the crypto world. It's what makes the market thrilling and potentially rewarding, but it's also what makes it unpredictable. With the right strategy, a cool head, and a sense of humor, you can ride out the swings and come out ahead.

Ready to level up? The next chapter dives deeper into tools and strategies for managing your crypto portfolio in a world that's always changing. Grab your popcorn—the adventure continues!

Crypto Investment Checklist:

- ✔☐ I've researched the whitepaper of my chosen cryptocurrency.

- ✔☐ I understand the risks associated with altcoins.

- ✔☐ I've diversified my crypto portfolio.

- ✔☐ I've set up a secure wallet.

Chapter 4: Accepting Crypto as Payment

Practical insights for modern businesses to embrace the digital revolution.

Imagine this: Your business gets a request from a customer who wants to pay for your services in Bitcoin. Do you say, "Sure!" and risk holding a volatile asset? Or do you scramble to figure out what a "blockchain" actually is? This chapter demystifies accepting cryptocurrency as payment, showing you how to navigate the process without losing your mind—or your money.

Practical Considerations: Accepting Crypto Without Losing Your Mind (or Money)

Accepting crypto payments may sound as futuristic as self-driving cars did a decade ago, but the future is now—and it's simpler than you think. This section will help you navigate the practical steps of getting started, choosing the right currencies, and safeguarding your business from crypto's infamous price rollercoasters.

Setting Up Crypto Payment Gateways

Options to Explore:
Think of crypto payment gateways as your digital cashiers. They

handle the behind-the-scenes complexity of blockchain transactions, making it as easy for you as swiping a credit card. Popular platforms like **Coinbase Commerce**, **BitPay**, and **NOWPayments** are designed to cater to businesses of all sizes.

- **Coinbase Commerce:** A user-friendly platform for businesses wanting to accept multiple cryptocurrencies, with seamless fiat conversion options.

- **BitPay:** Known for its robust security and flexibility, offering integrations for popular e-commerce platforms like Shopify.

- **NOWPayments:** Perfect for small businesses and freelancers, with low transaction fees and support for over 100 cryptocurrencies.

Real-World Example:
A coffee shop in Miami embraced Bitcoin payments using BitPay, attracting tech-savvy locals while sidestepping volatility by opting for auto-conversion to USD. Not only did they see increased customer loyalty, but they also saved on traditional credit card processing fees.

Steps to Implement:

1. **Choose Your Provider:** Consider transaction fees, supported cryptocurrencies, ease of integration, and whether you need automatic conversion to fiat currencies.

2. **Link Your Bank Account:** For businesses wanting stability, linking a bank account ensures smooth fiat conversions for instant liquidity.

3. **Update Checkout Systems:** Add crypto payment options to your website, POS system, or invoicing software. Bonus: Advertise this feature "We Accept Crypto" signs can attract a whole new demographic.

Pro Tip: Test the system with small, internal transactions before rolling it out to customers. There's no better way to learn than buying your own latte with Ethereum.

Choosing Which Cryptocurrencies to Accept

The Big Players:

- **Bitcoin (BTC):** The household name. Reliable but occasionally slow, like the family minivan of crypto.
- **Ethereum (ETH):** The tech-savvy option. Faster, but those gas fees can sting.
- **Stablecoins (USDC, USDT):** The financial equivalent of your grandma's cookies—steady, comforting, and never a surprise.

Pro Tip: Start simple. Accepting stablecoins like USDC minimizes volatility risks while keeping you in the crypto ecosystem. Over time, you can experiment with broader options as you gain confidence.

Managing Price Volatility

Crypto prices can move faster than your morning caffeine kick. One minute, Bitcoin's worth $60,000; the next, it's dropping faster than the Wi-Fi at your favorite café. Here's how to keep your revenue steady:

- **Set Up Auto-Conversion:** Many payment gateways allow you to convert crypto to fiat automatically at the point of transaction. This reduces the risk of holding onto assets that may lose value overnight.
    - *Example:* A boutique clothing store avoided headaches during Bitcoin's 2021 dip by enabling

instant USD conversion, ensuring stable cash flow despite market turbulence.

- **Establish Payment Policies:**
  - Offer crypto payments only for transactions over a specific value (e.g., $100+).
  - Incentivize stablecoin payments with small discounts—your customers win, and your balance sheet stays happy.

Pro Tip: Consider keeping a small portion of your crypto payments in their original form as a speculative asset. It's like playing the stock market but cooler (and possibly riskier). This aligns with our roadmap to financial freedom: leveraging innovative tools like crypto while safeguarding your cash flow for immediate needs.

Accounting and Taxes: Keep Uncle Sam Happy

While crypto payments feel futuristic, the IRS treats them like old-school property. Translation: every transaction is taxable. Here's how to stay on top of the paperwork without pulling your hair out:

Recording Transactions

Every crypto payment has two components:

- **The Sale:** Record the fiat value of the transaction (the price of your goods/services at the time of sale).
- **Capital Gains/Losses:** If you hold crypto and sell it later, track the difference between its original value and its selling price.

Tools for Tracking

Save yourself the stress of manually tracking wallet balances and tax implications:

- **QuickBooks with Crypto Integration:** Merges your crypto and fiat transactions into one seamless ledger.
- **CoinTracker:** Tracks gains, losses, and wallet activity across multiple platforms.

Tax Compliance

The IRS considers crypto payments a taxable event. Here's what you'll need to track:

- **Fair Market Value:** The dollar equivalent of the crypto payment at the time of sale.
- **Holding Periods:** If you hold crypto before selling, calculate capital gains or losses.

Pro Tip: Consult a CPA who specializes in crypto. If you don't have one yet, reach out to the Nealson Group, or find a professional who speaks fluent blockchain.

Legal and Regulatory Compliance: Playing by the Rules

Licensing and Permits

Some states or countries may require additional licenses to accept crypto. For example, New York's BitLicense is a strict regulatory framework for crypto businesses.

Complying with KYC/AML Rules

For B2B transactions, ensure you're compliant with **Know Your Customer (KYC)** and **Anti-Money Laundering (AML)** regulations. These safeguards prevent illicit activities like money laundering and fraud.

Pro Tip: Most payment processors include KYC/AML protocols, so you won't have to manage compliance manually.

Data Privacy Considerations

Storing customer wallet information? Be sure to follow privacy laws like **GDPR** (EU) or **CCPA** (California). Transparency is key—inform customers how their data will be used and secured.

Case Study: The Digital Café Experiment

"Beans & Blocks," a trendy coffee shop in Austin, Texas, took the leap into crypto payments and never looked back.

- **The Setup:** Using Coinbase Commerce, the café accepted Ethereum and USDC.
- **The Benefits:**
    - Avoided volatility with auto-conversion to USD.
    - Attracted crypto enthusiasts who spent 30% more per transaction.
    - Boosted their brand by aligning with tech-forward trends.

Feeling unsure about applying these strategies to your business? The Nealson Group specializes in guiding business owners through crypto adoption, cash flow planning, and financial strategy. Reach out to us at consultations@nealsongroup.com for tailored support.

Key Takeaway: Treating crypto as both a marketing opportunity and a payment method, "Beans & Blocks" grew their revenue by 40% in one year.

Is Accepting Crypto Right for Your Business?

Ask yourself these questions before diving into the crypto pool:

1. **Who are my customers?** Tech-savvy, global customers are prime candidates.

2. **What's my risk tolerance?** If market swings give you heartburn, stick to stablecoins or enable auto-conversion.

3. **Am I ready for compliance?** With the right tools and advisors, crypto complexity becomes manageable.

Chapter Wrap-Up

Accepting crypto payments isn't just a financial decision—it's a strategic move that can future-proof your business. By starting small, leveraging the right tools, and embracing the learning curve, you'll position your business as an innovator in a rapidly evolving digital economy.

Chapter 5: Decentralized Finance (DeFi): The New Frontier of Business Funding

What if I told you that the future of finance isn't in the banks or stock markets but on platforms powered by algorithms and smart contracts? Welcome to Decentralized Finance, or DeFi—a world where loans don't need banks, trading doesn't need brokers, and you, the business owner, have more financial control than ever before.

But don't worry; you don't need a degree in computer science to grasp DeFi. By the end of this chapter, you'll see how businesses like yours can use DeFi to borrow, lend, invest, and grow—all without a single bank visit.

What is DeFi? Breaking it Down

DeFi is like the financial world's cool younger sibling—decentralized, inclusive, and way more tech-savvy. It's a suite of financial services built on blockchain technology, replacing traditional intermediaries with self-executing smart contracts.

Key Features of DeFi:

- **Permissionless:** Anyone with an internet connection can participate—no credit scores or gatekeepers required.

- **Transparent:** All transactions are visible on the blockchain, ensuring accountability.
- **Borderless:** DeFi works globally, making it a great option for international businesses.

Real-World Analogy:

Imagine a lemonade stand. In traditional finance, you'd need a bank to give you a loan for lemons and a stockbroker to sell lemonade futures. In DeFi, you'd crowdfund directly from neighbors using a blockchain-based contract, cutting out all the middlemen.

DeFi in Action: Opportunities for Businesses

Lending and Borrowing: Tap Into Instant Liquidity

In the DeFi world, getting a loan is as easy as staking your crypto as collateral. Platforms like **Aave** and **Compound** let you borrow against your crypto holdings or lend your idle funds to earn interest.

How It Works:

1. You deposit collateral (e.g., Ethereum) into a DeFi platform.
2. Borrow stablecoins or other crypto at a fraction of the value of your collateral.
3. Repay the loan plus interest to retrieve your collateral.

Example Use Case:
A small e-commerce business needs $10,000 for inventory but doesn't want to sell its appreciating Bitcoin holdings. Using Aave, the owner stakes $15,000 worth of Bitcoin as collateral and borrows $10,000 in stablecoins to cover expenses, all without visiting a bank.

Example Use Case:
Imagine this: A boutique winery in Napa Valley faces a familiar seasonal challenge. Every spring, they need $20,000 for bottling, packaging, and labeling their new vintage. Traditionally, this meant

weeks of paperwork to secure a small business loan—often at unfavorable terms.

This year, the winery's owners decided to leverage their existing crypto holdings. They staked $30,000 worth of Ethereum on Aave, a popular DeFi platform, and borrowed $20,000 in USDC (a stablecoin tied to the U.S. dollar). The funds were available within minutes—no credit checks, no lengthy applications, and no bank fees.

By the time the new vintage hit shelves, the winery had generated $50,000 in sales. They used a portion of the proceeds to repay the loan and reclaim their Ethereum, which had appreciated in value during the bottling season.

The Outcome: The winery saved time and money compared to traditional financing methods. Additionally, their Ethereum holdings continued to grow as an investment, creating a win-win scenario.

Takeaway for Your Business: DeFi lending offers more than just convenience; it provides financial flexibility without sacrificing long-term assets. Whether you're managing seasonal costs, launching a new product line, or covering unforeseen expenses, platforms like Aave and Compound can act as your financial lifeline.

Key Benefits:

- Quick access to capital.
- No credit checks or paperwork.
- Retain ownership of appreciating assets.

Risks to Consider:

- Crypto price volatility could cause your collateral to drop below the required threshold, triggering liquidation.
- Always monitor loan-to-value ratios to avoid surprises.

Earning Interest: Put Idle Funds to Work

If your business has crypto sitting around, you can earn passive income by lending it out. DeFi platforms offer significantly higher yields than traditional bank accounts.

Example:

- A tech consulting firm with excess Ethereum deposits it on Compound and earns 5% annual interest, far better than any savings account.

Decentralized Exchanges (DEXs): Trade Without Intermediaries

DEXs like **Uniswap** and **SushiSwap** allow you to trade crypto assets directly with other users, bypassing centralized exchanges.

Why This Matters:

- For businesses accepting crypto payments, DEXs offer an easy way to convert less-used tokens into stablecoins or major cryptocurrencies like Bitcoin or Ethereum.
- No middlemen means lower fees and no delays.

Example Use Case:
A global freelance platform accepts payments in obscure altcoins. Using a DEX, they convert these into Ethereum with minimal fees and effort, maintaining their cash flow.

Liquidity Pools and Yield Farming: Advanced DeFi Strategies

Liquidity Pools:
Liquidity pools are the backbone of DeFi. Users contribute funds to these pools, enabling seamless trading on DEXs. In return, they earn a share of the transaction fees.

Example:

- A local brewery invests in a liquidity pool for the ETH/USDC trading pair. In return, they earn fees every time someone trades between those two currencies.

Yield Farming:
Yield farming is like the financial version of extreme couponing. By strategically moving your funds between DeFi platforms, you can maximize returns on your investments.

Example:

- A tech startup uses excess stablecoins to farm yields on Curve Finance, earning additional tokens that can be sold or reinvested.

Pro Tip: Yield farming is high-risk/high-reward. It's great for businesses with extra funds to experiment but not ideal for your emergency reserves.

The Risks and Rewards of DeFi

Rewards:

- **Access to Capital:** Borrow against your crypto without selling it.
- **Higher Returns:** Earn better yields on savings and investments.
- **Global Reach:** Participate in a financial system that works 24/7, across borders.

Risks:

- **Smart Contract Vulnerabilities:** Bugs in the code can lead to losses. Choose platforms that have undergone rigorous audits.

- **Market Volatility:** Collateral values can drop suddenly, risking liquidation.
- **Regulatory Uncertainty:** Governments are still catching up with DeFi's rapid growth.

Pro Tip: Only use well-known DeFi platforms with strong security reputations, like Aave, Compound, and Uniswap.

Case Study: The Global Manufacturer's DeFi Advantage

A mid-sized manufacturer based in Europe struggled with cross-border transaction fees and slow bank transfers. By adopting stablecoins and leveraging DeFi lending platforms, they:

- Borrowed $100,000 in USDC to purchase raw materials, saving thousands in interest compared to traditional loans.
- Used Uniswap to exchange local tokens for Ethereum, bypassing banks entirely.
- Improved cash flow while cutting transaction times from days to minutes.

Key Takeaway: DeFi helped the manufacturer stay competitive in a fast-moving market by reducing costs and increasing financial flexibility.

Is DeFi Right for Your Business?

Ask yourself:

1. **Do I have crypto assets or plan to accept them?** DeFi is ideal for leveraging crypto you already own.
2. **Can I tolerate risk?** While DeFi offers incredible opportunities, the risks require vigilance and financial literacy.

3. **Am I ready to learn?** A basic understanding of how DeFi works is crucial. But don't worry—your first smart contract doesn't need to be perfect.

Pro Tip: Start small. Test the waters with a lending or savings platform before diving into yield farming or advanced strategies.

Chapter Wrap-Up: Finance Without the Middlemen

DeFi is more than a buzzword—it's a financial revolution that empowers businesses to take control of their money. From borrowing and lending to trading and earning, the opportunities are vast for those willing to learn the ropes.

So, whether you're looking to cut out the banks, earn higher returns, or simply explore new possibilities, DeFi offers a roadmap to a decentralized financial future. Just remember: the early bird catches the worm, but the careful bird avoids the traps.

Questions for You:

1. Does your business have idle funds that could be earning interest through DeFi platforms?
2. What are the potential risks of using DeFi that concern you most, and how could you mitigate them?
3. Could borrowing against crypto assets provide a more flexible alternative to traditional loans for your business?

Chapter 6: NFTs and the Metaverse: Building Brands in the Digital Frontier

Imagine selling a product where the transaction doesn't end with ownership but extends into a digital relationship—offering exclusivity, loyalty perks, or a piece of art that lives forever on the blockchain. Welcome to the world of NFTs. Now, pair that with the Metaverse, where customers can step into a virtual storefront, interact with your brand, and experience something unforgettable. Together, NFTs and the Metaverse are transforming how businesses engage with customers and create value.

Understanding NFTs: More Than Digital Collectibles

NFTs, or Non-Fungible Tokens, are unique digital assets that prove ownership of items ranging from artwork to event tickets. What makes them powerful is their ability to create exclusivity and foster deeper connections with customers. Unlike cryptocurrencies such as Bitcoin or Ethereum, which are interchangeable, NFTs are one of a kind—think of them as the digital equivalent of a signed baseball card or a limited-edition collectible.

Businesses are increasingly tapping into NFTs for innovative branding strategies. Take, for example, a boutique fashion brand. By minting exclusive NFTs tied to limited-edition collections, they're not just selling clothing but offering their customers a piece of the brand's identity. These tokens can unlock early access to sales, invitations to special events, or even discounts on future purchases. For the customer, owning an NFT isn't just about the utility—it's about belonging to a community.

The potential doesn't stop there. Consider a fitness studio that mints NFTs as gym passes. Each pass comes with perks like personal training sessions or access to exclusive classes. This not only simplifies membership management but also provides customers with a tangible, tradable digital asset. It's a win-win for both businesses and their loyal followers.

How the Metaverse Redefines Engagement

The Metaverse is more than a buzzword; it's a shared virtual space where people interact as digital avatars. Think of it as a fusion of gaming, social media, and e-commerce, but on a much larger and more immersive scale. For businesses, this is the next frontier in branding and customer experience.

Picture a virtual storefront, beautifully rendered with your products on display. Customers can walk through, interact with items, and even make purchases—all from the comfort of their homes. Global luxury brands like Gucci are already capitalizing on this, with virtual spaces that attract younger, tech-savvy audiences eager for new experiences. These digital environments blur the line between physical and online shopping, offering engagement that's as entertaining as it is practical.

It doesn't end with retail. Events and experiences in the Metaverse are revolutionizing how brands connect with audiences. Imagine hosting a product launch or concert in a virtual space where attendees not only see the event but become part of it. Nike's "Nikeland" on Roblox is an example of this in action. Users can explore branded games, try on virtual sneakers, and interact with a community of fans, all while staying immersed in the brand's ecosystem.

NFTs and the Metaverse in Action: A Case Study

A global sneaker company recently made headlines by integrating both NFTs and the Metaverse into their customer strategy. First, they minted a series of limited-edition sneaker NFTs, each granting the holder early access to future collections. These NFTs quickly became status symbols, with customers flaunting their ownership both online and offline.

Next, they launched a virtual store in the Metaverse, where customers could try on digital versions of their sneakers and buy physical products directly. To top it off, the brand hosted a virtual concert featuring a chart-topping artist, accessible exclusively to NFT holders. The results were staggering: the NFTs sold out within hours, the concert generated widespread media attention, and online sales saw a 200% spike in the following month. This campaign demonstrated how combining these technologies can create unforgettable experiences while driving tangible business results.

Navigating the Challenges

Of course, adopting NFTs and entering the Metaverse isn't without its hurdles. For one, there's the technical learning curve. Minting NFTs or creating virtual spaces requires some technical expertise, though platforms like OpenSea, Decentraland, and The Sandbox simplify the process for beginners. Environmental concerns are another factor to consider, as blockchain transactions can be energy-intensive. Switching to eco-friendly blockchains like Polygon or Flow can address these concerns while maintaining performance.

Then there's the regulatory uncertainty. With governments still catching up to blockchain's rapid evolution, businesses must tread carefully when creating digital assets or virtual environments. Consulting with legal and financial experts is essential before diving in, especially for projects with significant monetary stakes.

Is It Right for Your Business?

Before jumping into NFTs or the Metaverse, ask yourself a few key questions. Do you have a tech-savvy audience? Younger generations and digital-first consumers are more likely to engage with these innovations. Does your brand thrive on creativity and visual appeal? Fashion, art, and entertainment are natural fits for these technologies, though industries like fitness and hospitality are quickly catching up. Finally, are you prepared to experiment? Success in these spaces requires a willingness to try new approaches, learn from mistakes, and adapt as the landscape evolves.

Chapter Wrap-up

NFTs and the Metaverse represent a shift in how businesses interact with their customers. These tools offer opportunities to create memorable experiences, build stronger communities, and unlock new revenue streams. Whether you're minting an NFT collection or opening a virtual storefront, the possibilities are endless for brands willing to explore the digital frontier.

As we move closer to a fully interconnected digital economy, the question isn't whether businesses should adopt NFTs or enter the Metaverse—but how soon they can embrace these exciting opportunities.

Chapter 7: Beyond Bitcoin: The Altcoin Explosion

Exploring other crypto assets and why diversification can be key.

Picture this: Maya, a small business owner, hears about Ethereum at a dinner party. Intrigued, she invests a modest $500. Over the next year, Ethereum's price soars, turning her initial investment into $3,000. Excited, Maya starts exploring other altcoins—some successful, like Solana, and others, like a meme coin hyped on social media, that plummet within weeks.

Maya's journey highlights the thrilling yet unpredictable world of altcoins. These alternatives to Bitcoin have reshaped the crypto landscape, offering opportunities for diversification, innovation, and, of course, risk. In this chapter, we'll dive into what makes altcoins unique, their real-world applications, and strategies to navigate this booming market.

Key Takeaway: The altcoin market is dynamic and full of potential, but success requires informed decisions and a healthy dose of caution.

Bitcoin might be the A-lister of the crypto world, but it's far from the only star on the stage. Enter altcoins: thousands of cryptocurrencies, each with its own quirks, powers, and, let's face it, drama. Think of Bitcoin as the headliner at a music festival—impressive, sure—but the altcoins are the eclectic side acts, each with its own flair, style, and sometimes questionable outfit choices.

This chapter dives into the ever-expanding universe of altcoins, giving you practical tips for navigating the market and showing why diversification can add more than just excitement to your portfolio.

What's in an Altcoin?

So, What Exactly Is an Altcoin?

Altcoins are any cryptocurrency that isn't Bitcoin. While Bitcoin paved the way, altcoins bring variety and innovation to the crypto world. They're like the supporting cast in a blockbuster franchise—sometimes underrated, sometimes overhyped, but always worth a look.

Altcoins fall into categories, each with its own personality:

- **Ethereum:** Often called the "silver" to Bitcoin's "gold," Ethereum is a platform for decentralized apps (DApps) and smart contracts. Think of it as the app store of crypto.
- **Stablecoins:** Coins like Tether (USDT) and USD Coin (USDC) are pegged to assets like the U.S. dollar, making them steady and boring—but in a good way.
- **Meme Coins:** The class clowns of crypto, these coins (e.g., Dogecoin and Shiba Inu) often start as jokes but can skyrocket with enough community hype.

The Shiba Inu Phenomenon

Shiba Inu, a meme coin with a cute dog mascot, went from being a joke to a sensation almost overnight. Created in 2020 by an anonymous developer, Shiba Inu marketed itself as the "Dogecoin Killer." Fueled by online communities and social media buzz, it gained massive popularity.

- **Example:** In October 2021, Shiba Inu spiked nearly 800% in value in a single month, proving that even a "joke" coin can bring serious returns. But like a rocket without a landing plan, what goes up fast can come down just as quickly.

Key Takeaway: Altcoins range from serious projects to meme-fueled phenomena. Coins like Shiba Inu prove that hype can lead to massive gains—but also wild risks.

Case Studies: Altcoins Changing the Game
1. **Ethereum**: Launched in 2015, Ethereum introduced the world to smart contracts—self-executing agreements coded on the blockchain. This innovation enabled decentralized applications (DApps), fueling industries like decentralized finance (DeFi) and NFTs (non-fungible tokens).
    - *Impact*: Platforms like Uniswap (a DeFi exchange) and OpenSea (an NFT marketplace) owe their existence to Ethereum's blockchain.
2. **Cardano**: Known for its focus on sustainability and academic rigor, Cardano uses a proof-of-stake model to process transactions with minimal energy consumption. It's been adopted for projects ranging from digital identity verification in Ethiopia to supply chain tracking.
3. **Solana**: Dubbed the "Ethereum killer," Solana boasts lightning-fast transaction speeds and low fees, making it ideal for decentralized gaming and NFT platforms.

Key Takeaway: Altcoins aren't just speculative assets—they're driving innovation and solving real-world problems.

Diversifying with Altcoins

Why Diversify with Altcoins?

Bitcoin might be the cornerstone of crypto, but relying solely on it is like eating pizza without any toppings—safe, but not nearly as fun. Diversifying with altcoins can provide growth potential, reduce risk, and add unique features to your portfolio.

The Pros:

1. **Higher Growth Potential:** Altcoins often start cheap, giving investors a chance at big returns.
    - **Example:** Early investors in Ethereum saw its value skyrocket from $1 in 2015 to over $4,000 in 2021.
2. **Different Use Cases:** Coins like Cardano focus on sustainability, while Polkadot connects multiple blockchains. Each has a unique purpose.
3. **Hedging Against Volatility:** Altcoins sometimes move independently of Bitcoin, providing balance during market swings.

The Cons:

1. **Higher Risk:** Many altcoins are even more volatile than Bitcoin, especially meme coins.
2. **Uncertain Futures:** Not all altcoins are built to last. Some projects fade out, taking your investment with them.

Key Takeaway: Altcoins can offer exciting opportunities but require careful research and a clear strategy.

Real-World Example: Shiba Inu's Wild Ride

Investors who treated Shiba Inu as a small, speculative play in a diversified portfolio enjoyed its explosive gains. Others who went all-in on the hype learned the hard way that meme coins can drop as fast as they rise. The lesson? A little fun is fine, but balance is key.

Navigating the Altcoin Jungle

How to Do Your Research on Altcoins

With thousands of coins out there, finding the right ones can feel like picking the best food truck at a festival. Here's how to separate the Michelin-starred projects from the mystery meat:

1. **Read the Whitepaper:**
   - A whitepaper is a coin's business plan. It should clearly explain the project's purpose, technology, and goals.
   - **Red Flag:** If it sounds vague or promises guaranteed riches, run.
2. **Check the Community:**
   - Strong online communities (like Shiba Inu's "ShibArmy") can signal grassroots support. But beware of pure hype—enthusiasm doesn't always equal substance.
3. **Look at the Team:**
   - Research the developers behind the project. Do they have credible backgrounds? Are they actively engaged? An anonymous team isn't necessarily bad, but transparency is always a plus.
4. **Evaluate the Market Cap:**
   - Coins with high market caps are usually more stable, while low caps offer higher risk but greater growth potential.

Resources to Help You Navigate

- **CoinMarketCap and CoinGecko:** Comprehensive sites for tracking prices, market caps, and trends.

- **Crypto News Sites:** CoinDesk and CoinTelegraph cover major developments and emerging projects.
- **Social Media:** Platforms like Reddit and Twitter are treasure troves of insight—but watch out for hype-driven advice.

Key Takeaway: Careful research is your best tool for finding promising altcoins. Don't let FOMO (fear of missing out) lead you astray.

Key Strategies for Altcoin Investing

1. **Start Small:** Allocate a small portion of your portfolio to speculative altcoins.
2. **Set Clear Goals:** Know when to take profits and when to cut your losses.
3. **Stay Grounded:** Trends come and go; focus on projects with real potential.

Tips for the Crypto Newbie (Because We've All Been There)

Starting out in crypto can feel like you've just joined a book club where everyone else has already read the book *and* the sequel. But don't worry—here's how to keep up without faking it:

1. **Start with the basics:** Master Bitcoin and blockchain before diving into flashy trends like NFTs or DeFi. Otherwise, it's like running before you can walk—and no one wants to trip over a digital wallet.
2. **Diversify your sources:** Don't believe everything you read on one site (or subreddit). Crypto is like a buffet—sample widely before committing to the sushi that *might* be questionable.
3. **Be patient:** Rome wasn't built in a day, and neither is your crypto knowledge. Stick with it, and soon you'll be the one explaining "hash rates" at brunch.

Chapter Wrap-Up

Bitcoin might be the gateway to crypto, but altcoins are where the adventure begins. From serious projects like Ethereum to the wild world of meme coins, the altcoin market offers something for everyone—if you know how to navigate it.

While Shiba Inu's rise shows that anything is possible in the crypto world, successful investing requires more than just hope. With careful research, diversification, and a healthy dose of skepticism, you can explore the altcoin jungle without getting lost.

Ready to dive into Part 2 of the book? In the next section, we'll shift gears from crypto to cash flow, exploring how to manage your finances in a digital-first world. Let's keep building your financial toolkit—one step at a time!

Questions For You:

1. Have you considered diversifying into altcoins? If so, what criteria would you use to evaluate potential investments?
2. How comfortable are you with the risks associated with altcoins, and what steps could you take to manage those risks?
3. Which emerging trends in altcoins align with your business goals or personal financial strategy?

Bonus Materials

Here's a curated list of **books, articles, tools, and podcasts** tailored to the cryptocurrency section of your book:

Books

1. **Mastering Bitcoin** by Andreas M. Antonopoulos
   - A comprehensive guide to Bitcoin, blockchain technology, and cryptocurrency fundamentals.
2. **The Bitcoin Standard** by Saifedean Ammous
   - Explains Bitcoin's role as "sound money" and its potential to disrupt traditional finance.
3. **Blockchain Basics** by Daniel Drescher
   - Ideal for beginners, this book breaks down blockchain concepts into easy-to-understand explanations.
4. **Cryptoassets: The Innovative Investor's Guide to Bitcoin and Beyond** by Chris Burniske and Jack Tatar
   - Focuses on evaluating and investing in cryptocurrencies and blockchain projects.
5. **DeFi and the Future of Finance** by Campbell R. Harvey
   - Explores decentralized finance and how it is revolutionizing the financial industry.

Articles

1. **"The Basics of Bitcoins and Blockchains"** on Investopedia
   - Covers fundamental concepts like mining, wallets, and blockchain.
2. **"A Beginner's Guide to Cryptocurrency"** on CoinDesk
   - Provides a broad introduction to cryptocurrency, from buying your first coin to understanding market trends.
3. **"How Blockchain Technology Works"** on MIT Technology Review
   - A high-level overview of blockchain technology and its applications.
4. **"Ethereum vs. Bitcoin: What's the Difference?"** on Decrypt
   - Explains key distinctions between these two major cryptocurrencies.

5. **"Stablecoins: What They Are and Why They Matter"** on CoinTelegraph
   - Explores the growing role of stablecoins in the crypto ecosystem.

Tools

1. **CoinMarketCap**
   - A popular tool to track cryptocurrency prices, market capitalization, and trends.
2. **Etherscan**
   - A blockchain explorer for Ethereum, allowing users to track transactions and wallet activity.
3. **Ledger Live**
   - A companion app for Ledger wallets to manage cryptocurrencies securely.
4. **Messari**
   - A research tool for in-depth insights and analysis on cryptocurrency projects.
5. **DeFi Pulse**
   - Tracks decentralized finance projects and total value locked (TVL) in DeFi protocols.

Crypto Cash Flow Toolkit

Managing cash flow in a digital-first world requires the right tools. Whether you're navigating traditional finance or integrating cryptocurrency into your operations, these resources can streamline your efforts:

- **Coinbase Commerce:** Accept crypto payments seamlessly, with options to automatically convert funds into fiat currency, reducing volatility risks.
- **QuickBooks with Crypto Integration:** Track both crypto and fiat transactions, offering a unified view of your finances.
- **CoinTracker:** Simplify crypto portfolio tracking and tax calculations for businesses accepting or holding digital assets.

- **Float:** A forecasting tool for creating accurate cash flow projections, even when handling both fiat and crypto inflows.
- **CryptoTaxCalculator:** Handle tax implications of your business's crypto transactions effortlessly.
- **BitPay:** A robust payment platform that enables crypto acceptance while offering conversion features.
- **Treasury Prime:** Integrates crypto treasury management tools for businesses looking to balance digital and traditional financial strategies.
- **Trezor and Ledger Wallets:** Secure hardware wallets for protecting long-term crypto reserves offline, reducing cybersecurity risks.
- **DeFi Pulse:** Monitor decentralized finance platforms, ideal for short-term liquidity solutions or financing options in crypto.

Podcasts

1. **Unchained** with Laura Shin
   - A must-listen podcast featuring industry leaders discussing cryptocurrency, blockchain, and the future of finance.
2. **The Pomp Podcast** with Anthony Pompliano
   - Covers macroeconomic trends, Bitcoin, and blockchain innovation.
3. **Crypto 101**
   - A beginner-friendly podcast that explains cryptocurrency and blockchain topics in simple terms.
4. **Bankless**
   - Focuses on decentralized finance (DeFi) and Ethereum, with actionable insights for crypto enthusiasts.
5. **What Bitcoin Did** with Peter McCormack
   - Explores Bitcoin's impact on the economy and society through expert interviews.

Beginner's Crypto Toolkit: Your Survival Guide

Before you go full "crypto bro" or start calling everything a "blockchain revolution," check out these beginner-friendly tools to level up your game:

- **CoinDesk:** For when you want to sound smart at meetings.
- **Decrypt:** For when you want to actually understand what you're talking about.
- **Messari & CoinMarketCap:** For diving deeper into the rabbit hole.
- **Khan Academy:** For free, no-nonsense learning.
- **Reddit:** For the memes (and some decent advice if you can spot it).

Bridging the Gap: Crypto and Cash Flow

While crypto offers thrilling opportunities for innovation and investment, it's not a silver bullet for managing your business's day-to-day operations. Crypto might capture headlines, but cash flow keeps the wheels turning. It's the unsung hero that ensures your business can adapt, grow, and survive any economic climate. In the next section, we'll shift gears and dive into how to master the lifeblood of any business—cash flow—while leveraging the insights gained from exploring the digital frontier.

Bridging the Digital and the Practical: Crypto Meets Cash Flow

As we wrap up our exploration of cryptocurrency, it's clear that crypto isn't just a speculative asset or a buzzword—it's a transformative tool for modern businesses. But even with all its innovation, crypto is only one side of the financial coin. On the other side lies the unglamorous yet essential world of cash flow management. No matter how revolutionary your tech or forward-thinking your strategies, a business runs—or stumbles—on cash flow. In the next section, we'll marry the dynamic potential of cryptocurrency with the tried-and-true principles of cash flow management, ensuring your business isn't just riding the wave of innovation but staying afloat when the tide changes.

PART 2: Cash Flow

*Think of this section as a crypto-enhanced sequel to **Cash Flow Cure**. We'll revisit some tried-and-true principles of cash flow management and explore how they evolve in the context of digital assets and blockchain. Crypto might be exciting, but let's get real—cash flow is what pays the bills. In this section, we'll revisit timeless cash flow strategies and show how they evolve in a world where digital currencies are changing the game.*

Chapter 8: Profit's a Liar – Why Cash Flow Is the Real King

Uncovering the mystery of cash flow and why it's your business's lifeline.

So, you're crushing it in business—sales are through the roof, your product is hotter than Taylor Swift tickets, and your P&L statement is a work of art. You're ready to pop champagne and start Googling "luxury yachts for beginners." But then, you log into your bank account and see... crickets. Your balance is emptier than a beach in a hurricane.

What gives? Welcome to the perplexing (and slightly infuriating) world of cash flow, where profits are theoretical, and cash is king.

In a world where cryptocurrencies are gaining traction, cash flow management faces new hurdles. Businesses accepting crypto payments must manage price volatility, transaction delays, and conversion to fiat currencies—all of which impact liquidity. While profits may soar on paper due to asset appreciation, real-world cash flow could falter if crypto assets aren't immediately liquidated or converted.

If this sounds familiar, it might be because we talked about this in my first book, *Cash Flow Cure*. There, I called cash flow the "heartbeat" of your business—and I stand by it. This chapter builds on those fundamentals, diving deeper into why cash flow is so essential, how it differs from profit, and how to avoid the pitfalls that could leave you stranded.

Interactive Exercise: Analyzing Crypto's Cash Flow Impact
Imagine your ecommerce store accepts payments in Bitcoin. You sell $10,000 worth of goods today, but Bitcoin's value drops 10% before you convert it to cash. Meanwhile, your suppliers demand payment in fiat currency within seven days.

Questions:

- How does the delay in conversion affect your cash flow?
- What strategies could you use to mitigate risks of crypto volatility?

Tip: Diversifying payment methods and setting up automated crypto-to-fiat conversions can reduce risk.

Now, let's unravel the mystery of cash flow and ensure that yacht dream doesn't turn into a rubber dinghy reality.

Cash Flow vs. Profit Explained

Why They're Not the Same

Profit and cash flow are like Instagram vs. reality. Profit looks great in photos—shiny, promising, dressed to impress. Cash flow? That's the messy, real-life version that decides if you can actually pay the bills.

Profit:
Profit is the MVP of your income statement. It's the number left after you subtract expenses from revenue. It's what makes investors nod approvingly and your accountant feel warm and fuzzy inside. But profit doesn't always mean cash in hand—it includes sales on credit, depreciation, and other non-cash items that look good on paper but won't help you pay the electric bill.

- **Example:** You sell $50,000 worth of products but allow customers 90 days to pay. That profit looks stellar, but unless they pay up quickly, your bank account might still be crying for mercy.

Cash Flow:
Cash flow is the real-world hero. It's the actual cash moving in and out of your business. Think of profit as the charming dinner guest who makes a great impression but conveniently forgets their wallet. Cash flow is the friend who shows up with cash in hand to split the check.

Positive cash flow means you can pay bills, reinvest, and maybe even splurge on that espresso machine for the office. Negative cash flow? That's the financial equivalent of digging through your couch cushions for gas money.

- **Example:** It's like your personal finances. Your paycheck might look impressive, but if it's already spoken for by bills, groceries, and your "self-care" Amazon purchases, you're not exactly rolling in cash.

The Credit Card Illusion

Profit is like swiping your credit card for an epic shopping spree.

You look great walking out of the store, but the bill eventually comes due. Cash flow is what happens when you check your bank account and realize your card payments are eating into your dinner fund.

Key Takeaway: Profit shows potential, but cash flow shows reality. Both are important, but cash flow is what keeps the lights on and the payroll checks from bouncing.

For a detailed exploration of these fundamentals, see Chapter 2 of **Cash Flow Cure**, where I dive into the mechanics of why profit can look good on paper but leave your bank account gasping for air.

Meet "Digital Brew Co.," a trendy café in Austin, Texas, that became the talk of the town by accepting crypto payments. On launch day, they sold $12,000 worth of coffee and muffins—but here's the twist: half of it was paid in Ethereum. Excited by their success, the owners decided to hold onto their crypto, hoping its value would rise.

One week later, Ethereum's value dipped by 15%, turning that $6,000 worth of crypto into $5,100. Meanwhile, their landlord wasn't interested in Bitcoin or blockchain; they wanted fiat. The café scrambled to sell their Ethereum during a market slump, losing even more value in transaction fees.

The lesson? Crypto might be an exciting payment option, but cash flow management requires balancing innovation with stability. Holding crypto is fine—but always keep a portion liquid to meet immediate expenses.

Interactive Exercise: Analyze Your Cash Flow

Let's put theory into practice! Here's a simple scenario to work through:

Scenario:

You're running a hipster café called 'Beans & Beards.' Last month, you sold $15,000 worth of artisanal lattes, but half your customers are 'still waiting for payday.' Meanwhile, your baristas want their checks yesterday.

Questions:

1. What's your profit for the month? (Spoiler: It's not what you think.)
2. What's your cash flow situation?
3. How could you tactfully convince those freeloading latte lovers to pay up faster?

Write down your answers before moving on to the next section. This exercise will help you see the practical implications of cash flow management.

Cash Flow's Role in Business Health

Cash Flow: The Fuel for Your Business Engine

Imagine your business is a race car. Profit is the flashy engine, but cash flow is the fuel line. Even the most powerful engine won't get you across the finish line if the fuel line is leaking.

- **Example:** During the early days of a global pandemic, countless profitable businesses ran out of cash and shuttered because they didn't have the liquidity to cover payroll or rent.

Liquidity: The Lifeline You Didn't Know You Needed

Liquidity is your ability to turn assets into cash quickly. It's the difference between having a Picasso painting (valuable but illiquid) and a wallet full of cash (less glamorous but ready to use).

- **Example:** A small business owner with $500,000 tied up in inventory might look rich on paper but could struggle to pay a $5,000 supplier bill if they don't have enough cash on hand.

Cash Flow Powers Growth

Positive cash flow isn't just about survival—it's about seizing opportunities. Want to hire that rockstar developer, buy new equipment, or launch a killer marketing campaign? Cash flow is what makes those dreams a reality.

Key Takeaway: Cash flow is the lifeblood of your business. It fuels daily operations, helps you weather storms, and gives you the flexibility to grow.

Recognizing the Warning Signs

Even the most successful businesses can fall into cash flow traps. Let's shine a light on these pitfalls before they trip you up:

The Overgrowth of Expenses

It starts innocently—new office furniture here, upgraded software there. Before you know it, you've got a fancy espresso machine no one knows how to use and a corporate retreat budget that rivals a wedding. Expenses multiply, and your cash flow suffers.

- **Solution:** Conduct regular expense audits. Do you really need five premium software subscriptions when one will do?

The Accounts Receivable Swamp

Your invoices are piling up, and customers are taking their sweet time paying. Your profit says you're golden, but your bank balance is sinking.

- **Solution:** Tighten payment terms, offer discounts for early payments, and chase down late payers with the determination of a dog after a bone.

The Inventory Avalanche

Your warehouse is packed to the brim with unsold products. Your cash is tied up, and those items aren't getting any fresher.

- **Solution:** Optimize inventory levels using demand forecasting. Avoid overstocking, even if it's tempting to buy in bulk.

The Sales Slump Quicksand

Sales slow, but expenses stay steady. The result? Your cash reserves drain faster than a kiddie pool in July.

- **Solution:** Diversify revenue streams and build an emergency fund for lean months.

The Unexpected Disaster Pit

A supplier goes under, a major client cancels, or your roof leaks—whatever the crisis, it derails your cash flow.

- **Solution:** Maintain a financial buffer and invest in business insurance to weather these storms.

When Your Invoices Go on Vacation

There's nothing quite like sending out invoices and hearing... nothing. Crickets. Silence. It's like your clients decided to backpack through Europe with your payment.

Here's how to keep your receivables from taking extended holidays:

1. **Send Friendly Reminders:** Think of it as a polite nudge, like saying, "Hey, your payment is overdue, but I still like you!" Automated tools can do this without making you seem like a loan shark.
2. **Charge Late Fees:** Nothing speeds up payments like a tiny nudge in the form of a penalty. But keep it reasonable—this isn't a mob movie.
3. **Offer Payment Plans:** Make it easy for clients to pay in chunks if they're facing financial hiccups. It's better to get $500 now than wait six months for $5,000.

Pro Tip: Always have a backup plan for non-payers, whether it's a collection agency or offering barter deals. (Yes, you'll take two crates of their artisanal jams as partial payment if it means cash flow!)

Key Takeaway: Cash flow pitfalls can strike anywhere, but with vigilance and proactive management, you can navigate around them. Recognizing the warning signs early is the key to keeping your business on solid financial footing.

Real-World Examples: The Impact of Cash Flow

1. **Success Story**:
    - A bakery in Austin, Texas, used cash flow management to thrive during a tough season. By offering discounts for early customer payments and negotiating with suppliers for longer terms, they

turned a potential cash crunch into a growth opportunity.
2. **Cautionary Tale**:
    o A tech startup in Silicon Valley went bankrupt despite high profits. Why? They relied too heavily on accounts receivable, and delayed payments from clients left them without enough cash to cover payroll and rent.

Key Takeaway: Managing cash flow isn't just about numbers—it's about survival. Even a profitable business can fail without sufficient cash on hand.

Chapter Wrap-Up

Profit might steal the spotlight, but cash flow is the unsung hero of your business. It's what keeps your doors open, your team paid, and your stress levels manageable. Understanding the difference between profit and cash flow, maintaining liquidity, and avoiding common pitfalls can mean the difference between thriving and just surviving.

Ready to dive deeper? The next chapter will guide you through practical strategies to optimize your cash flow and set your business up for long-term success. Because while yachts are nice, a business that pays its bills is even better.

Questions For You:

1. How frequently do you review your cash flow compared to your profit statements? Could you benefit from a more regular cadence?
2. If your largest client delayed payment by 30 days, how would it impact your ability to meet your financial obligations?
3. What steps could you take today to ensure your cash flow remains positive during a downturn?

Chapter 9: Cash Flow Strategies for the Modern Business: Show Me the Money!

Tips and tricks to keep cash moving and avoid common pitfalls.

In business, cash is like oxygen: you don't think about it until it's running out. And let's be honest—when your cash flow is tight, it can feel like a slow-motion chokehold. The good news? There are strategies to keep the money moving, avoid the most common cash flow killers, and even create breathing room for growth.

This chapter is your guide to mastering cash flow in today's fast-paced, digital-first world. Whether you're chasing overdue invoices, trimming unnecessary expenses, or deciding whether to use short-term financing, these strategies will help you keep the lights on, the team paid, and your sanity intact.

And if this feels like a continuation of *Cash Flow Cure*, you're not wrong. That book laid the groundwork, but here, we're leveling up with fresh insights and tools for modern businesses. So buckle up—it's time to show cash flow who's boss.

Tips and Tricks to Keep Cash Moving

Speed Up Incoming Cash

Crypto-Specific Cash Flow Tips

- **Enable Automated Conversions**: Use tools like Coinbase Commerce or BitPay to instantly convert crypto payments to fiat. This minimizes the impact of market volatility on your cash flow.
- **Accept Stablecoins**: Unlike Bitcoin or Ethereum, stablecoins like USDC or DAI are tied to fiat currencies, offering price stability. Accepting these ensures your receivables maintain their value.
- **Use Smart Contracts for Payments**: In B2B transactions, smart contracts can automate payment terms and escrow funds, ensuring timely payouts.

Getting paid faster isn't just a nice-to-have—it's a necessity. Here's how to keep the cash flowing in:

- **Offer Incentives for Early Payments:** Discounts for paying invoices early can encourage customers to move your bill to the top of their to-do list.
    - **Example:** Offer a 2% discount if customers pay within 10 days instead of 30. It's a small price to pay for faster cash flow.
- **Get Paid Upfront When Possible:** For services or custom orders, request a deposit or full payment before you start.

Delay Outgoing Cash

- **Negotiate Payment Terms:** Work with suppliers to extend payment terms from 30 days to 45 or 60 days.
    - **Example:** Many large retailers negotiate longer payment terms to hold onto their cash longer. There's no reason your business can't do the same.
- **Stagger Expenses:** Time your payments to align with when cash comes in. This reduces the risk of running short at critical moments.

Key Takeaway: The faster money comes in and the slower it goes out, the healthier your cash flow will be. It's not rocket science—it's just good business. For crypto payments, the same rule applies, but with a twist: speed up inflows by automating conversions, and slow outflows by negotiating longer fiat payment terms while keeping crypto reserves stable.

Step-by-Step Guide: Negotiating Payment Terms with Vendors

1. **Review Current Terms**: Identify which vendors offer the shortest payment terms (e.g., net 30).
2. **Assess Your Needs**: Decide how much extra time you'd like—net 45 or net 60 terms can provide breathing room.
3. **Prepare Your Case**: Highlight your payment history and explain why extended terms would strengthen your partnership.
    - *Example*: "By extending payment terms, I can better manage inventory costs and place larger orders with you."
4. **Negotiate Strategically**: Offer a compromise if needed (e.g., smaller upfront payments with longer terms).
5. **Document the Agreement**: Always formalize changes in writing to avoid misunderstandings.

Outcome: Negotiating payment terms can improve cash flow without adding new costs to your business.

Resource: Cash Flow Tools You Can Use

- **Cash Flow Projection Template**: Plan your monthly cash inflows and outflows to anticipate shortages or surpluses. *[Send me an email at consultans@nealsongroup.com and I'll send you a free template]* Columns for expected revenue, fixed costs, variable costs, and net cash flow. Fill in actual amounts to compare projections vs. reality.

- o   *Tip*: Regularly update this template to reflect changes in your business.
- **Expense Audit Checklist**: Streamline your spending by reviewing all costs. *[Send me an email at consultans@nealsongroup.com and I'll send you a free template]*:
  - o   Identify recurring expenses (e.g., subscriptions).
  - o   Prioritize spending on ROI-generating activities.
  - o   Eliminate redundant tools or services.

Pro Tip: Save time by using digital tools like Google Sheets or apps like QuickBooks to automate these processes.

The Art of Receivables: Keeping Cash Flow Strong

Receivables can be tricky—they look great on your profit statement, but if they're not collected, they're just IOUs. Managing receivables effectively is like herding cats: frustrating, but absolutely essential.

Tighten Your Payment Terms

- **Keep Terms Clear and Short:** Instead of offering "Net 30," consider reducing terms to "Net 15" or even requiring partial upfront payments.

Follow Up Without Fear

Don't be shy about reminding customers that their payment is due. A polite but firm approach keeps your receivables moving.

- **Example:** Use automated invoice reminders. Services like QuickBooks and Xero can send gentle nudges that say, "Hey, pay me!" without you having to pick up the phone.

The Friendly-but-Firm Approach

Think of it as channeling your inner kindergarten teacher: kind, but with an unyielding resolve. Friendly emails, followed by firmer notices if necessary, are the key to keeping the relationship intact while getting paid.

Key Takeaway: Collections don't have to be a battle—be proactive, consistent, and firm without losing your cool.

Expense Management: Reducing Costs Without Sacrificing Quality

Cutting costs doesn't mean you have to compromise your standards or become the office Scrooge. Smart expense management is about making your money work harder, not cutting corners.

Audit Your Subscriptions

- **Review Monthly Charges:** Check your business bank account for recurring charges you've forgotten about. Do you really need five graphic design software subscriptions when you only use one?

Renegotiate Contracts

- **Suppliers and Vendors:** Ask for better rates or discounts. It's amazing how often a simple request can save you money.

Automate Where Possible

Automation can save both time and money. Tools like automated email responders, payroll systems, and inventory trackers can reduce the need for additional staff while keeping your operations running smoothly.

Outsource Strategically

Hiring full-time staff for every task can be costly. For specialized projects or short-term needs, consider outsourcing to freelancers or agencies.

- **Example:** A small ecommerce business might hire a part-time bookkeeper instead of a full-time accountant, saving on salary and benefits.

Key Takeaway: Expense management isn't about being cheap; it's about being smart. Regularly review, renegotiate, and optimize to keep costs under control.

Short-Term Financing Options: When and How to Use Credit Wisely

Sometimes, you need a cash flow boost to get through a tough spot or seize an opportunity. Short-term financing can help—but only if you use it wisely.

Business Lines of Credit

A line of credit gives you flexible access to funds when you need them. It's like having a financial safety net you only use in emergencies.

- **Example:** Use a line of credit to cover payroll during a slow season, then pay it off when cash picks up.

Invoice Financing

If receivables are dragging down your cash flow, consider invoice financing. This allows you to get an advance on unpaid invoices, giving you cash now instead of waiting.

- **Example:** If you're waiting on a $10,000 invoice that's due in 30 days, invoice financing could provide up to 90% of that amount immediately (minus fees).

Credit Cards: Friend or Foe?

Credit cards can be a useful tool but should be handled with caution. Use them for short-term needs only, and pay them off quickly to avoid high-interest charges.

Crowdfunding and Peer-to-Peer Loans

For businesses with creative projects or strong customer followings, crowdfunding can be a way to generate cash without traditional debt.

- **Example:** A bakery might use Kickstarter to pre-sell holiday gift boxes, generating cash upfront to fund production.

Key Takeaway: Financing can be a lifesaver or a trap—choose options carefully, and always have a plan for repayment.

Practical Insights: Proven Cash Flow Tips

Drawing from industry wisdom and real-world examples, here are strategies that financial experts often recommend:

1. **Diversify Revenue Streams**

- *Advice*: Diversification is a buffer against cash flow shocks. Don't depend on one major client or product.
- *Example*: A manufacturing company stabilized its cash flow by adding a subscription-based maintenance service to its products.

2. **Leverage Automation**
   - *Advice*: Use tools to manage receivables, schedule follow-ups, and track invoices. Automation reduces human error and ensures nothing is overlooked.
   - *Example*: Businesses using invoice automation software report faster payments and fewer overdue accounts.

3. **Strategic Financing**
   - *Advice*: Short-term financing, like lines of credit or invoice factoring, should be seen as a bridge—not a crutch. Always have a repayment plan.
   - *Example*: A startup avoided payroll delays during a lean month by leveraging invoice financing, ensuring employee morale stayed high.

Key Takeaway: By combining diversification, automation, and strategic financing, you can create a resilient cash flow system for your business.

Tools for Cash Flow and Crypto Management

Here are some tools to help you manage cash flow effectively, whether you're dealing with fiat or crypto:

- **Coinbase Commerce**: Accept crypto payments with instant conversion to fiat to avoid volatility.
- **QuickBooks with Crypto Integration**: Track crypto payments alongside traditional financial records.
- **CoinTracker**: Simplifies crypto tax reporting and portfolio management.

- **Float**: A forecasting tool for cash flow projections, perfect for businesses combining fiat and crypto.
- **CryptoTaxCalculator**: For calculating tax implications of crypto transactions in business.
- **DeFi Pulse**: Tracks decentralized finance platforms, useful for businesses using DeFi for short-term financing.

Chapter Wrap-Up

Managing cash flow isn't just about crunching numbers—it's about creating a strategy that keeps money moving in and out of your business in a way that works for you. Whether it's speeding up receivables, cutting unnecessary expenses, or using short-term financing wisely, the goal is to create a cash flow system that's as smooth as your best sales pitch.

As we've learned, cash flow isn't just the lifeblood of your business; it's the foundation for growth, stability, and even a little peace of mind. And if you want to dive even deeper, *Cash Flow Cure* has plenty more tricks to help you master the art of keeping cash in your business where it belongs.

Now, let's gear up for the next chapter, where we'll explore how to take your healthy cash flow and use it to create long-term financial freedom. Because let's face it—building a business is great, but building a life you love is the ultimate goal.

Chapter 10: Avoiding Cash Flow Crunches: How to Stay Liquid in a Digital World

Lessons in liquidity that even the biggest companies sometimes forget.

Alright, business owners, let's talk cash flow—the MVP of your financial game plan, the fuel that keeps your entrepreneurial engine running. In the last chapter, we covered cash flow strategies to keep your business thriving. Now, we're shifting gears to tackle something every business faces at some point: the dreaded cash flow crunch.

Picture this: sales are rolling in, your profit margins are healthy, and then BAM—a surprise expense hits, or a key client delays payment. Suddenly, your bank balance looks like a tumbleweed town in an old Western. What do you do? This chapter is your guide to navigating those tricky moments, from forecasting like a pro to building financial safety nets that can weather any storm.

Whether you're a startup juggling slim margins or a seasoned business aiming to avoid liquidity hiccups, these strategies will keep your cash flowing like a well-synced Spotify playlist. Let's dive in!

Forecasting and Budgeting: Preparing for Seasonal Fluctuations

Know Thy Financial Seasons

Forecasting becomes more nuanced when cryptocurrency is involved. Seasonal trends in revenue are now compounded by market trends in crypto valuations. For instance, a sudden market dip could reduce the value of your receivables, while a bull run might inflate your holdings without improving liquidity. Businesses must account for these fluctuations by maintaining a reserve in stablecoins or fiat.

- **Tip: Protect Against Crypto Volatility** Use "trigger conversions" with automated crypto wallets to sell assets when their value drops below a certain threshold. This ensures you maintain enough liquid cash flow for operating expenses.

Every business has its ups and downs—summer might be a goldmine for ice cream shops, but it's a slow crawl for ski resorts. Understanding your financial seasons is step one to avoiding cash flow crunches.

- **Tip:** Use historical data to identify patterns. If revenue dips in certain months, plan ahead to stockpile cash during the good times.
    - **Example:** A landscaping company might save a portion of its summer earnings to cover winter slowdowns.

The Rollercoaster of Seasonal Business

Seasonal cash flow is like riding a rollercoaster blindfolded—thrilling when revenue spikes and terrifying when it plummets.

Example: A lawn care business rakes it in during summer but winters? Not so much. You don't want to end up selling your snowblower just to make payroll.

Here's how to stay strapped in:

1. **Build a War Chest:** Save a portion of your peak-season earnings to cover off-season expenses. Treat it like a squirrel hoarding nuts for winter.
2. **Diversify Your Offerings:** The lawn care business can offer snow shoveling or holiday light installations in winter. Find complementary services to balance the seasons.
3. **Hire Seasonally:** Consider temp workers or contractors for peak months to avoid paying year-round salaries.

Key Takeaway: With planning, you can keep the thrills of seasonal business without the stomach-churning drops.

Budgeting: Your Financial Roadmap

Think of your budget as a GPS for your business. Without it, you're just guessing which financial turns to take.

- **Break it Down:** Separate your expenses into fixed (rent, utilities) and variable (supplies, marketing).
- **Plan for Surprises:** Set aside 5–10% of your monthly budget for unexpected costs—it's like packing an extra pair of socks for a trip, just in case.

Key Takeaway: Forecasting and budgeting help you anticipate cash flow gaps before they happen, so you're not scrambling when slow seasons hit.

Emergency Funds for Businesses: How Much to Set Aside

Why Every Business Needs a Safety Net

An emergency fund isn't just a luxury; it's a necessity. From equipment breakdowns to surprise tax bills, unexpected expenses can hit when you least expect them.

- **Example:** During the early days of the COVID-19 pandemic, businesses with emergency funds weathered the storm far better than those without.

How Much is Enough?

The rule of thumb is three to six months' worth of essential operating expenses. For lean startups, aim for at least three months; for established businesses, six months or more provides extra security.

- **Breakdown:**
    - Rent, utilities, and payroll? Yes.
    - Fancy office snacks? Maybe not.

Build it Gradually

Don't feel pressured to save it all at once. Allocate a small percentage of monthly revenue to your emergency fund until you hit your target.

Key Takeaway: An emergency fund is your business's financial parachute. Build it gradually, and when the unexpected happens, you'll be ready to land safely.

Automating Cash Flow Monitoring: Tools and Tech for

Tracking Liquidity

Why Automation is a Game-Changer

Manual cash flow tracking is about as fun as untangling holiday lights. Automation not only saves time but also reduces errors and gives you real-time insights.

- **Example:** A restaurant owner using QuickBooks Online can track daily cash flow, identify slow weeks, and adjust inventory orders accordingly—all without lifting a pen.

Tools to Keep Cash Flow in Check

1. **Accounting Software:** QuickBooks Online, Xero, or FreshBooks can automate invoicing, track expenses, and reconcile accounts with ease.
2. **Forecasting Platforms:** Apps like Float or Pulse predict future cash flow based on past trends, giving you a financial crystal ball.
3. **Payment Integration:** Pair systems like Stripe or Square with your accounting software to streamline collections and get paid faster.

Benefits of Automation

- **Real-Time Updates:** Always know where you stand financially.
- **Error Reduction:** No more late nights correcting spreadsheet typos.
- **Time Savings:** Focus on growth, not grunt work.

Key Takeaway: Automating cash flow monitoring gives you a bird's-eye view of your finances while freeing up time to focus on strategy.

Navigating Short-Term Financing: Friend or Foe?

When Financing Makes Sense

Sometimes, borrowing money isn't a sign of failure—it's a smart way to smooth out cash flow. Short-term financing can help bridge the gap during lean times or fund growth opportunities.

Options to Consider

1. **Lines of Credit:** Flexible and accessible, these work well for covering short-term gaps.
   - **Example:** Use a line of credit to pay suppliers during a seasonal lull, then repay it when revenue picks up.
2. **Invoice Financing:** Sell unpaid invoices to a lender for immediate cash.
   - **Example:** A consulting firm waiting on a $20,000 invoice could get $18,000 upfront (minus fees) through invoice financing.
3. **Short-Term Loans:** Great for specific projects or purchases but should be repaid quickly to avoid high-interest costs.
4. **Crowdfunding:** Ideal for creative projects or customer-funded ventures, letting you generate cash without traditional debt.

Proceed with Caution

Not all financing is created equal. High-interest rates or rigid repayment terms can turn a helpful loan into a financial nightmare.

Key Takeaway: Short-term financing can be a lifesaver—just ensure you understand the terms and have a plan for repayment.

Interactive Tool: Cash Flow Risk Assessment Quiz

Take this quick quiz to identify areas of potential risk in your cash flow management. Score yourself on each question (1 = Never, 3 = Sometimes, 5 = Always).

Questions:

1. Do you regularly monitor your cash flow using projections?
2. Do you have an emergency fund that covers at least three months of operating expenses?
3. Are your receivables consistently collected within agreed payment terms?
4. Do you negotiate payment terms with suppliers to align outflows with inflows?
5. Are you confident in your ability to manage unexpected expenses without financial strain?

Results:

- **20–25 Points**: Your cash flow management is strong—keep up the good work!
- **15–19 Points**: You're on the right track, but consider tightening processes in specific areas.
- **Below 15 Points**: It's time to focus on improving cash flow strategies to avoid potential crunches.

Success Stories: Lessons from the Field

1. **The Coffeehouse Comeback**:
   A small coffee shop in Portland faced cash flow crunches during the pandemic. By introducing prepaid gift cards and negotiating rent deferrals, they stayed afloat and eventually thrived when restrictions lifted.

2. **Tech Startup Resilience**:
   A SaaS company struggling with long receivable cycles used invoice factoring to maintain liquidity. This enabled them to retain staff and launch a key product update that doubled their revenue.
3. **E-commerce Efficiency**:
   An online retailer implemented cash flow forecasting software and discovered they were overstocking inventory. By optimizing purchase cycles, they freed up $20,000 in working capital.

Key Takeaway: Strategic planning and proactive management can turn potential crises into opportunities for growth.

Chapter Wrap-Up

Avoiding cash flow crunches isn't about luck; it's about preparation and smart management. By forecasting seasonal trends, building an emergency fund, automating cash flow monitoring, and using financing wisely, you can keep your business liquid and ready for anything.

As we've seen, cash flow is the heartbeat of your business. Keeping it steady means, you can navigate challenges, seize opportunities, and focus on growth without constantly looking over your shoulder.

Ready for the next step? In the next chapter, we'll look at how to transition from managing cash flow to building true financial freedom. Because staying liquid is great, but creating wealth that works for you? That's the ultimate goal.

What to Do Next:

1. Research crypto-friendly payment gateways.
2. Calculate your business's cash flow for the past 3 months.
3. Set up a contingency fund for volatile market periods.

Chapter 11: From Red to Black: Getting Your Cash Flow in the Positive

A practical guide to boosting cash flow for business stability.

Alright, cash flow crusaders, we've tackled the fundamentals, dodged the pitfalls, and learned how to keep cash moving. But what if your cash flow isn't just sluggish—it's in the red, bleeding out faster than a broken vending machine on free soda day? Fear not, because this chapter is your financial triage guide.

We're diving into the heart of cash flow issues to diagnose, treat, and ultimately fix them. Whether you're a startup trying to stay afloat or an established business battling a rough patch, these strategies will help you stop the financial bleeding and get back on the path to profitability. Think of this as the final level in the cash flow game—let's get your business from surviving to thriving.

Assessing Financial Health: Diagnosing Cash Flow Issues

Before you can fix cash flow problems, you need to figure out what's causing them. Think of this step as putting your business through a financial checkup—you can't treat what you don't understand.

The Telltale Signs of a Cash Flow Crisis

Look out for these red flags:

- **Stale Invoices:** Unpaid invoices piling up? That's a clogged financial artery.
    - **Example:** A digital marketing agency waiting months for client payments might look profitable on paper, but their bank balance tells a different story.
- **Shrinking Bank Balance:** A consistently draining account is like a bathtub with the drain open—eventually, you're left high and dry.
- **Credit Card Overload:** Using credit cards to pay for everyday expenses? That's duct-tape finance—useful in a pinch but not a long-term fix.
- **Payment Juggling:** Delaying payments to cover others is a financial house of cards.
- **Sleepless Nights:** If cash flow worries are keeping you up, it's time to act. Trust that gut feeling—it's usually spot on.

Digging Deeper: Financial Detective Work

To diagnose cash flow issues, you need to do some serious sleuthing:

- **Analyze Your Cash Flow Statement:** It's your business's diary, showing you exactly where money is coming from and where it's leaking out.
- **Calculate Key Metrics:**
    - **Operating Cash Flow Ratio:** Are your core operations generating enough cash to cover expenses?
    - **Cash Conversion Cycle:** How long does it take for a dollar spent to come back as a dollar earned?
- **Conduct an Expense Audit:** Find those sneaky costs draining your resources—whether it's unused software subscriptions or an overpriced office coffee habit.

- **Scrutinize Sales Cycles:** Are there seasonal dips or customer behavior changes you can anticipate? Knowing when revenue dips can help you plan cash reserves better.

Key Takeaway: Diagnosing your cash flow issues is like finding the source of a leak. Once you know where the problem is, you can stop the flow and start repairs.

Stopping the Bleeding: Quick Fixes for Cash Flow Crises

If your business is waiting on large crypto payments, consider using crypto-backed invoice financing platforms. These allow you to borrow against receivables held in digital assets, providing instant liquidity.

Liquidity isn't optional; it's the lifeline of your business. For businesses accepting crypto, converting a portion of your holdings into fiat reserves ensures you always have cash on hand to cover immediate needs.

Speed Up Inflows

- **Collect Receivables Faster:** Send invoices immediately and follow up regularly. Use technology to automate reminders and make it easier for customers to pay.
    - **Example:** A graphic design firm might use tools like FreshBooks to cut invoice lag time in half.
- **Offer Discounts for Early Payments:** Incentives like 2% off for paying within 10 days can motivate customers to settle invoices faster.
- **Pre-Sell Products or Services:** Selling subscriptions or gift cards upfront brings in cash before expenses hit.

Slow Down Outflows

- **Negotiate Payment Terms:** Ask suppliers for longer terms—extending from 30 to 60 days can free up cash when you need it most.
- **Cut Non-Essentials:** Tighten up your budget by eliminating unnecessary expenses like underused software or pricey office perks.

Short-Term Financing Options

- **Use Lines of Credit Wisely:** A line of credit can be a lifeline in a crunch—just make sure you have a repayment plan.
- **Consider Invoice Financing:** Get upfront cash for unpaid invoices without waiting for client checks.

Key Takeaway: Quick fixes can stabilize your cash flow in the short term, buying you time to implement long-term solutions.

Building a Long-Term Cash Flow Strategy

Diversify Revenue Streams

Relying on one source of income is risky. Expanding your offerings can create a safety net.

- **Example:** A bakery might add online cake classes or delivery services to boost revenue year-round.

Tighten Cash Flow Processes

- **Forecast Regularly:** Use tools like Float or Pulse to predict cash flow and plan for dips.
- **Create a Rolling Budget:** Update your budget monthly to reflect real-time changes in income and expenses.

Build a Cash Reserve

Once you've stabilized, aim to set aside three to six months of operating expenses. This reserve acts as a buffer against future downturns.

Key Takeaway: Long-term strategies ensure your cash flow stays positive, even during tough times.

Success Stories: Turning Cash Flow Positive

1. **The Boutique Retailer's Revival**
   - A small fashion boutique in Miami faced negative cash flow due to overstocking inventory. By using a cash flow forecasting tool and negotiating flexible terms with suppliers, they reduced their monthly outflows by 20%. Within four months, they reported a positive cash flow for the first time in two years.
2. **The SaaS Startup's Pivot**
   - A software startup was on the brink of shutting down due to long receivable cycles. They introduced a subscription-based payment model, which brought consistent cash inflows. This shift not only stabilized cash flow but increased their customer retention rate by 30%.
3. **The Freelancer's Strategy**
   - A freelance graphic designer struggled with inconsistent payments. By requesting upfront deposits and offering a discount for early payments, they eliminated overdue invoices and maintained steady cash flow, even during slower months.

Key Takeaway: Small, deliberate changes can make a significant difference in your cash flow health, ensuring your business thrives in any environment.

Final Push to the Positive

Mindset Matters

Getting your cash flow back in the black isn't just about numbers—it's about mindset. Think of cash flow as the pulse of your business. Keeping it strong means making smart, proactive decisions daily.

Celebrate Small Wins

Every time you close a big invoice, cut an unnecessary cost, or hit a cash flow goal, take a moment to celebrate. Progress is progress, and each step brings you closer to long-term stability.

Create a Cash Flow Culture

Involve your team in cash flow management. Teach them to value efficiency, minimize waste, and recognize the importance of timely payments. A financially aware team can make a big difference.

Key Takeaway: A positive cash flow isn't just a destination—it's a way of running your business every day.

Final Thoughts on Cash Flow

As we wrap up this section on cash flow, let's take a moment to reflect. You've learned to:

- Differentiate between profit and cash flow.
- Anticipate and navigate cash flow challenges.
- Use tools, techniques, and strategies to keep cash moving.

- Build a foundation for long-term stability and growth.

Cash flow might not be the flashiest part of business, but it's the one that keeps everything else running. With the right strategies in place, you're not just surviving—you're building a business that's resilient, adaptable, and ready for whatever comes next.

Now that your cash flow game is strong, it's time to shift focus. In the next section, we'll dive into creating financial freedom—because a healthy business is just the beginning. The ultimate goal is building a life you love. Let's make it happen.

From Surviving to Thriving: Cash Flow as a Gateway to Freedom

Mastering cash flow isn't just about surviving the financial ups and downs of running a business; it's about laying the foundation for something far greater—financial freedom. Every decision to optimize cash flow, every strategy to manage digital and traditional transactions, is a step toward creating a business that supports your dreams rather than limits them. For a deeper dive into cash flow strategies and essential metrics, check out my book *The Cash Flow Cure*—it's packed with even more tools and insights to help you take control of your financial future.

In the final section, we'll connect the dots between financial discipline and the ultimate goal: a life where your business works for you, enabling choices and opportunities aligned with your values.

Part 3: Financial Freedom

Helping readers turn their crypto understanding and cash flow strategies into true financial independence.

Chapter 12: Financial Freedom: More Than Just a Buzzword

What financial freedom really means for business owners—and why you should care.

Building a business is no small feat. It takes grit, determination, and a willingness to learn from every curveball thrown your way. But as important as day-to-day operations are, they're not the endgame. The ultimate goal is financial freedom—a place where your business isn't just surviving but thriving, and where you're not just working for money but making money work for you.

Financial freedom isn't a cliché or a pipe dream. It's a tangible goal that business owners can achieve by aligning their finances with their values, goals, and aspirations. It's about turning the cash flow strategies you've mastered into a springboard for independence.

This chapter dives into what financial freedom means for business owners, how it differs from financial security, and how you can cultivate a mindset that moves you closer to achieving it. Let's unpack the possibilities and pave the path toward a future where your business fuels the life you want—not the other way around.

Create Your Financial Freedom Vision

Financial freedom isn't just about numbers—it's about living the life you've always imagined. To make this vision tangible, take a moment to personalize it:

1. **Vision Board**: Collect images, quotes, or symbols that represent your goals. Maybe it's a beach house, the freedom to travel, or simply more time with loved ones. Display this board where you'll see it daily.
2. **Journal Exercise**: Write a journal entry as if you've already achieved financial freedom. Answer these questions:
    - What does your typical day look like?
    - How do you feel knowing your financial life is in control?
    - What have you been able to achieve with this freedom?

Pro Tip: Revisit your vision board or journal regularly to keep your goals front and center.

Defining Financial Freedom—What It Means for Business Owners

Financial freedom is a versatile concept. For some, it's the ability to retire early and travel the world. For others, it's about flexibility—choosing when and how they work. For business owners, financial freedom often means having the security to navigate uncertainties and the ability to make decisions without being constrained by finances.

The Power of Choice

At its core, financial freedom is about control—control over your time, decisions, and priorities. Imagine having the ability to take a month off to travel, invest in a passion project, or say no to a high-maintenance client. It's about steering your business and your life where you want to go, not where you're forced to go.

- **Example:** A business owner with steady cash flow and diversified income streams might decide to work four days a week to spend more time with family. That's financial freedom in action.

Security as a Foundation

Financial freedom isn't about reckless spending; it's about knowing you're covered if the unexpected happens. Whether it's a market downturn, a global pandemic, or a sudden equipment breakdown, having a financial safety net means you can handle challenges without derailing your goals.

- **Example:** Companies that built robust cash reserves before COVID-19 adapted faster than those living paycheck to paycheck.

Flexibility and Work-Life Balance

For many business owners, financial freedom means breaking free from the traditional 9-to-5 grind. It's about creating a business that aligns with your life, not the other way around.

Passion Meets Purpose

Financial freedom allows you to focus on what truly matters—whether that's giving back, investing in personal growth, or exploring new opportunities. It's the difference between running a business to survive and running a business to thrive.

Key Takeaway: Financial freedom is a mix of choice, security, flexibility, and purpose. It's the result of intentional decisions that align your business with your personal and financial goals.

Financial Freedom vs. Financial Security—Understanding the Difference

While financial freedom and financial security are closely related, they serve distinct roles in your journey.

Financial Security: The Foundation

Think of financial security as the base layer of financial freedom. It's about having enough to cover your needs and weather unexpected storms. It includes:

- **Emergency Funds:** Covering 3–6 months of expenses.
- **Debt Management:** Reducing liabilities to manageable levels.
- **Insurance:** Protecting yourself with health, life, and business coverage.
- **Savings:** Building a financial cushion for the future.

Financial Freedom: The Goal

Financial freedom builds on security, providing the resources and flexibility to make decisions aligned with your values. It's about having options—whether that means pursuing passion projects, scaling your business, or retiring early.

- **Example:** Financial security is paying off your mortgage; financial freedom is owning multiple properties that generate passive income.

Key Takeaway: Financial security is your safety net, while financial freedom is your launching pad. Both are essential, but freedom is the ultimate goal.

Building a Freedom Mindset

Financial freedom starts in your mind. Cultivating the right mindset can make the difference between feeling stuck and creating meaningful progress.

Embrace Abundance

A scarcity mindset focuses on limitations: "What if I run out of money?" An abundance mindset focuses on possibilities: "What can I create with what I have?" This shift opens the door to opportunities, collaboration, and innovation.

- **Example:** Business owners with an abundance mindset invest in growth, even during uncertain times, knowing the long-term payoff outweighs the short-term risk.

Focus on Value

Instead of chasing money, focus on providing value. The businesses that succeed in the long run are those that solve real problems and deliver lasting impact.

- **Example:** A CPA firm offering value-added services like financial coaching attracts loyal clients who see the partnership as an investment, not a cost.

Practice Gratitude

Gratitude amplifies perspective. Instead of fixating on what's missing, focus on what's working. This mindset can improve decision-making and build resilience.

Align Actions with Goals

Every decision, big or small, should bring you closer to your vision of financial freedom. Whether it's reinvesting profits, building passive income streams, or automating operations, alignment is key.

Key Takeaway: A freedom mindset combines gratitude, value creation, and alignment with an abundance outlook. It's the mental framework that propels you toward independence.

Connect Through Meditation: My Personal Practice

I've found that meditation is one of the most powerful tools for achieving clarity and staying focused on my goals. I personally meditate for 5–10 minutes almost every day, and it has been life-changing.

To help you connect with your financial freedom vision, try this guided exercise:

1. **Find a Quiet Spot**: Sit comfortably, close your eyes, and take a few deep breaths.
2. **Visualize Your Future**: Imagine what financial freedom looks and feels like for you. Picture the people, places, and experiences that define your ideal life.
3. **Set Your Intention**: Repeat this affirmation: "I am creating financial freedom with every decision I make."

If you'd like a more structured approach, below are steps I personally use. Use it to deepen your connection to the financial freedom mindset.

Step 1: Prepare Your Space *(2 minutes)*

1. Find a quiet, comfortable spot where you won't be disturbed.

2. Sit or lie down in a relaxed position. You can use a meditation cushion or chair for support.
3. Dim the lights or light a candle to create a calming atmosphere.

Optional: Play soft instrumental music or nature sounds in the background.

Step 2: Focus on Your Breath *(3 minutes)*

1. Close your eyes and take three deep breaths. Inhale through your nose for four counts, hold for four counts, and exhale slowly through your mouth for six counts.
2. Let your breathing return to a natural rhythm. Focus on the sensation of the air entering and leaving your body.

As you breathe, allow your mind to quiet and your body to relax.

Step 3: Visualize Your Financial Freedom *(6–8 minutes)*

1. Picture yourself in a future where you've achieved financial freedom. Visualize the following:
    - **Your Daily Life**: Where are you? What does your ideal day look like? Are you working on projects you love, spending time with family, or traveling?
    - **Your Environment**: Picture the details. What colors, sounds, and textures surround you? Are you on a beach, in your dream home, or in a bustling city?
    - **Your Feelings**: How do you feel in this moment? Experience the sense of peace, joy, and security that comes with financial independence.
2. As you continue this visualization, repeat silently or aloud:
    - "I am free to live the life I choose."
    - "My financial decisions align with my highest goals."
    - "I am in control of my financial future."

Step 4: Anchor the Vision *(2 minutes)*

1. Take a mental snapshot of this visualization. Imagine locking this image into your mind as a source of motivation and focus.
2. Slowly bring your attention back to the present. Wiggle your fingers and toes, and when ready, open your eyes.

Step 5: Reflect and Journal *(Optional)*

After the meditation, spend a few minutes writing down what you saw, felt, and experienced during the exercise. This reflection can serve as a powerful reminder of your goals.

Questions For You:

1. What does financial freedom mean to you, and how would achieving it change your life or business?
2. What specific steps could you take in the next 90 days to move closer to your financial goals?
3. Are there areas in your financial plan where incorporating digital tools like crypto or blockchain could add value?

Final Thoughts

Financial freedom isn't a pipe dream reserved for tech moguls or hedge fund managers. It's a goal within reach for business owners who approach it with intention and strategy. By combining the solid foundation of financial security with a mindset focused on growth and possibility, you can turn your business into the engine that powers your ideal life.

In this last section of the book, we'll explore actionable strategies to make financial freedom your reality—starting with the systems, tools, and habits that can help you build wealth and take control of your financial future. Because at the end of the day, your business should serve you, not the other way around.

Chapter 13: Creating a Financial Freedom Roadmap: Destination Independence

Step-by-step planning to reach your ultimate business and financial goals.

Congratulations! You've navigated the intricate worlds of cryptocurrency, mastered the art of cash flow, and developed a mindset primed for financial freedom. Now, it's time to bring it all together and create a roadmap to your ultimate destination: financial independence.

This chapter isn't about vague platitudes or lofty dreams. It's about creating a clear, actionable plan tailored to your goals. Financial freedom isn't something you stumble upon—it's something you design, step by step. Think of this as your GPS for life, guiding you through detours, traffic, and open highways toward the future you envision. Let's get started.

Setting Financial Goals—Long-Term Planning for Wealth

Defining your financial goals is the first step to turning dreams into reality. Without a destination in mind, it's impossible to chart a course.

Envision Your Financial Dreamscape

Close your eyes and imagine your ideal life. Do you see yourself managing a business remotely while traveling? Funding passion projects? Building a legacy? Financial goals start with a clear vision of what success looks like for you.

- **Example:** Elon Musk reinvested earnings from selling his first company to fund SpaceX and Tesla. His financial goals weren't just about wealth—they were aligned with his vision of advancing technology and sustainability.

Set SMART Goals

SMART goals (Specific, Measurable, Achievable, Relevant, Time-Bound) provide a practical framework for success: *(The concept of SMART goals (Specific, Measurable, Achievable, Relevant, Time-Bound) was introduced by George T. Doran in 1981, providing a practical framework for goal setting and success.)*

- **Specific:** Define precise goals, like saving $500,000 for retirement or paying off a loan by 2028.
- **Measurable:** Use benchmarks to track progress, such as reaching $100,000 in investments by next year.
- **Achievable:** Be ambitious but realistic. Stretch goals are motivating; impossible ones are discouraging.
- **Relevant:** Ensure goals align with personal values and business aspirations.
- **Time-Bound:** Add deadlines to create urgency and accountability.

Build Goal Hierarchies

Break big dreams into smaller, actionable steps. For example:

- **Ultimate Goal:** Achieve $1 million in net worth by 2030.
- **Short-Term Goals:** Save $20,000 annually, invest 15% of profits, and eliminate high-interest debt by 2025.

Key Takeaway: Goals create the structure for your financial future. Whether it's funding your child's education, building a dream home, or achieving total financial independence, SMART goals make it tangible.

Steps to Financial Independence—Practical Moves for a Freedom-Based Future

Reaching financial independence requires disciplined action, not just good intentions. These steps help bridge the gap between your present and your goals.

Budget Like a Boss

Your budget is the foundation of your financial roadmap. It allocates resources to priorities and reveals opportunities to save or invest.

- **Example:** Tech entrepreneur Sarah Blakely famously saved startup funds by cutting personal expenses and reinvesting profits from her first sales into expanding Spanx.

Destroy Debt

High-interest debt is a wealth killer. Create a repayment plan that prioritizes high-interest accounts first while maintaining minimum payments on others.

Save Strategically

Automate savings to ensure consistency. Use high-yield savings accounts for emergency funds and set aside money for specific milestones.

Invest Wisely

Diversify your portfolio with stocks, bonds, real estate, or even crypto. Understand your risk tolerance and consider professional advice when needed.

- **Example:** Warren Buffett began investing as a teenager, leveraging compounding returns to grow his wealth.

Build Passive Income Streams

Generate income without constant effort through rentals, dividend-paying stocks, or online businesses. This reduces dependence on active income and accelerates independence.

Passive Income: Spoiler Alert, It's Not Always Passive

Passive income gets hyped up like the holy grail of financial freedom. "Make money while you sleep!" sounds dreamy, right? But here's the kicker—most passive income streams require an *active* effort to set up.

Examples That Sound Passive (but aren't):

- **Real Estate Investing:** Sure, renting properties sounds hands-off—until you're fixing a leaky toilet at 2 a.m. or chasing a tenant who "forgot" to pay.
- **Dividend Stocks:** Buying shares is easy, but monitoring market trends and staying calm during downturns takes nerve (and caffeine).
- **Online Courses:** Yes, you can sell your knowledge while binging Netflix, but creating that course? Hours of prep, filming, and editing. (Hope you like hearing your own voice on repeat.)

Key Takeaway: Passive income is awesome, but don't let the "passive" part fool you. It takes upfront work, maintenance, and sometimes a good plumber. The good news? Once you set it up, it truly does become the financial gift that keeps on giving.

Protect with an Emergency Fund

A solid emergency fund is your financial armor. Aim for 3–6 months of expenses in a liquid account to weather unexpected challenges.

Key Takeaway: Financial independence is a marathon, not a sprint. It requires discipline, intentionality, and consistent action over time.

Monitoring and Adjusting the Plan—Staying on Course

Even the best plans need adjustments as life evolves. Monitoring progress and recalibrating ensures you stay on track toward your goals.

Track Progress Regularly

Review budgets, savings, and investments quarterly. Track key metrics like net worth and income growth to stay aligned with your roadmap.

Course-Correct When Needed

Life happens—markets shift, opportunities arise, and priorities change. Adapt by reassessing your goals and strategies regularly.

- **Example:** During the 2008 financial crisis, many businesses pivoted, cutting costs and realigning strategies to survive and later thrive.

Celebrate Milestones

Acknowledge progress to stay motivated. Whether it's paying off a credit card or reaching your first $10,000 in savings, every win matters.

Keep Learning

Stay informed about market trends, investment opportunities, and financial strategies. Lifelong learning ensures your financial plan remains relevant in a changing world.

Key Takeaway: Financial planning is dynamic. Regular reviews and adjustments keep you aligned with your evolving goals and circumstances.

Questions For You:

1. If your industry became fully digital within five years, would your business be ready to adapt?
2. What digital tools or strategies could you start exploring today to future-proof your operations?
3. How could adopting blockchain or cryptocurrency enhance your current business model?

Final Thoughts: Your Roadmap to Freedom

Financial freedom is not about luck—it's about intentional planning, disciplined action, and staying adaptable. You've laid the groundwork by mastering cryptocurrency, cash flow, and a financial freedom mindset. Now, with a clear roadmap, you're equipped to turn dreams into reality.

As you close this book, remember: financial independence is not just a destination but a journey. Celebrate the progress, learn from the setbacks, and keep moving forward. Your business is not just a tool for generating income; it's the vehicle that will carry you to the life you envision.

Here's to your financial freedom and the limitless possibilities ahead.

Conclusion

Conclusion: Your Next Steps to Financial Freedom

Congratulations on reaching the end of this guide!

You've journeyed through the intricate worlds of cryptocurrency, cash flow management, and financial freedom, gaining knowledge, tools, and strategies to take control of your business and finances.

Whether you laughed at a joke, nodded at a key insight, or scribbled a note to yourself in the margins, the goal was to inspire action and confidence.

Let's Recap

Here are the biggest takeaways from our time together:

Crypto isn't just hype—it's an opportunity: Understanding cryptocurrency can unlock new possibilities for your business.

With a cautious yet open approach, you can use it as a tool for growth and diversification.

Cash flow is king: No matter how successful your business seems on paper, cash flow determines its survival.

Mastering cash flow management ensures stability and opens doors for opportunities.

Financial freedom is achievable: It's not a fantasy reserved for the ultra-wealthy—it's a goal that any business owner can reach with the right mindset, planning, and persistence.

Your Next Steps

This isn't the end of your financial journey; it's the beginning of a new chapter.

Now's the time to:

Put knowledge into action: Review the chapters that resonated most and start implementing changes.

Remember, even small adjustments can make a big difference over time.

Keep learning: The financial world evolves, and staying informed is crucial.

Whether it's following cryptocurrency trends, exploring new cash flow tools, or fine-tuning your financial independence plan, continuous growth is key.

Ask for help when needed: You don't have to go it alone.

As a CPA with years of experience, I know the value of expert advice when navigating financial challenges.

The Big Picture: Crypto, Cash Flow, and Freedom

As we prepare for an increasingly digital future, remember that the path to financial freedom isn't a sprint—it's a marathon of thoughtful decisions and consistent actions. Crypto can be a powerful tool in your arsenal, but it's your ability to manage cash flow, adapt to trends, and set clear financial goals that will define your success. This isn't just about staying afloat in a changing economy; it's about thriving and building the life you've envisioned. The future is digital, and your business is ready to meet it head-on.

Final Thoughts

Financial freedom isn't about hitting a jackpot or chasing the next trend—it's about creating a business and a life that align with your values and dreams.

It's about making intentional decisions that lead to stability, independence, and opportunities to do what matters most to you.

So, here's to your success. To your growth. To the business you're building and the future you're creating.

The journey doesn't stop here—because the best financial stories are the ones we write ourselves. Let's make yours extraordinary.

Now go out there, make bold moves, and never forget: the road to financial freedom is paved with determination, humor, and a solid plan.

Here's to your next adventure!

Warm regards, Christopher O'Neal, CPA, MBA The Nealson Group

Resource Materials

Here's a curated list of top resources for financial planning across books, apps, tools, websites, and podcasts to help with budgeting, investing, and achieving financial independence:

Books

1. **The Millionaire Next Door** by Thomas J. Stanley and William D. Danko
    - Insights into building wealth through disciplined spending and smart financial choices.
2. **Your Money or Your Life** by Vicki Robin and Joe Dominguez
    - A step-by-step guide to transforming your relationship with money and achieving financial independence.
3. **Rich Dad Poor Dad** by Robert Kiyosaki
    - A classic book explaining the importance of financial education and investing.
4. **I Will Teach You to Be Rich** by Ramit Sethi
    - Practical, no-nonsense advice on budgeting, saving, and automating finances.
5. **Broke Millennial** by Erin Lowry
    - Tailored to younger audiences, this book explains financial basics and overcoming common challenges.

Apps and Tools

1. **YNAB (You Need a Budget)**

- A budgeting app that helps you plan for every dollar and stick to your financial goals.
2. **Mint**
    - A free app for budgeting, tracking expenses, and monitoring credit scores.
3. **Personal Capital**
    - Combines budgeting tools with investment tracking to provide a holistic financial view.
4. **Fidelity Retirement Score**
    - Helps you assess whether you're on track for retirement and suggests actions to improve.
5. **Morningstar**
    - A trusted resource for researching and tracking investments, including mutual funds and ETFs.

Websites and Blogs

1. **NerdWallet**
    - Offers tools, reviews, and calculators for budgeting, credit cards, and investing.
2. **Investopedia**
    - Comprehensive financial education resource covering everything from beginner investing to advanced financial strategies.
3. **Mr. Money Mustache**
    - A blog focused on the FIRE (Financial Independence, Retire Early) movement.
4. **The Simple Dollar**
    - Offers practical advice on managing money, paying off debt, and saving for the future.
5. **SmartAsset**
    - Provides calculators and tools for tax planning, home buying, and retirement saving.

Podcasts

1. **ChooseFI**
   - Real-life stories and strategies for achieving financial independence and retiring early.
2. **The Dave Ramsey Show**
   - Practical advice on budgeting, getting out of debt, and managing finances.
3. **Afford Anything** by Paula Pant
   - Focuses on the philosophy of money, freedom, and creating a life you love.
4. **The Stacking Benjamins Show**
   - A lighthearted take on personal finance, featuring expert guests and practical tips.
5. **Money For the Rest of Us**
   - Explains how money works and provides insights on investing and financial planning.

Online Courses

1. **Financial Peace University (Dave Ramsey)**
   - A comprehensive course on budgeting, saving, and getting out of debt.
2. **Udemy: Personal Finance Courses**
   - Offers a range of affordable courses on topics like investing, retirement planning, and budgeting.
3. **Coursera: Financial Planning for Young Adults (University of Illinois)**
   - A free course designed to teach financial basics for young professionals.

Bonus Section: Exploring the Frontiers of Crypto and Finance

Introduction

Welcome to the "level-up" zone! You've mastered the essentials of cryptocurrency, cash flow, and financial freedom, but the digital economy is constantly evolving. This bonus section is where we go from *crypto curious* to *crypto Jedi*. Packed with advanced strategies, global insights, and future-proof tactics, this section will ensure you're not just surviving in the digital age—you're thriving.

As you prepare for a more digital future, take the first step with confidence. Feeling unsure about applying these strategies to your business? The Nealson Group specializes in guiding business owners through crypto adoption, cash flow planning, and financial strategy. Reach out to us at consultations@nealsongroup.com for tailored support.

Chapter 14: Advanced Crypto Strategies

Behavioral Finance and Risk Psychology

"When you stop learning, you start losing." – Anonymous Crypto Enthusiast

Welcome to the advanced playbook for making your crypto work harder, smarter, and with fewer sleepless nights. This chapter dives into strategies for managing risk, earning passive income, and navigating the thrilling chaos of the crypto market like a seasoned pro.

Behavioral Finance and Risk Psychology

Ever wondered why you keep checking your portfolio every five minutes, even though you told yourself to "HODL and chill"? That's behavioral finance at work, where your emotions and biases mess with your strategy. Here's how to outsmart your inner FOMO.

Common Pitfalls

1. **FOMO (Fear of Missing Out):** You hear a coworker made 10x on Shiba Inu, and suddenly, you're buying meme coins during your lunch break.
   Solution: Set a rule: No crypto buys during emotional spikes. Use limit orders instead of impulsive market orders.
2. **Panic Selling:** Prices drop 20%, and your gut screams, "SELL EVERYTHING!"
   Solution: Look at historical charts. Volatility is the norm, not the exception. Create stop-loss orders to automate decision-making.
3. **Overtrading:** Chasing the next big thing leads to excessive trades and skyrocketing fees.
   Solution: Stick to a diversified strategy and trade only when it aligns with your goals.

Case Study: The Calm HODLer vs. The Emotional Trader

In 2021, Sarah bought $10,000 worth of Ethereum and decided to "set it and forget it." Meanwhile, her friend Tom bought the same amount but traded aggressively during market dips. A year later, Sarah's holdings grew to $25,000, while Tom barely broke even after fees and mistimed trades. Lesson? Sometimes doing nothing is the smartest move.

Advanced DeFi Strategies

DeFi (Decentralized Finance) is where crypto geeks and money nerds unite to bypass traditional banks and unlock new earning potential. Here's how to join the revolution without losing your shirt.

Yield Farming: High Risk, High Reward

Yield farming is like planting a money tree—but one that needs constant watering and comes with a manual in 12 languages. By staking or lending your crypto, you can earn rewards from DeFi platforms like Aave, Curve, or Yearn Finance.

- **How It Works:**
    1. Deposit your crypto into a liquidity pool (think of it as a community savings account).
    2. Earn rewards in the form of interest or additional tokens.
    3. Reinvest or withdraw—your choice.
- **Pro Tip:** Always check the APY (annual percentage yield) and the platform's security audits before committing.

Case Study: The Bakery Staking Success

A small bakery in Portland, Oregon, set aside $10,000 from holiday sales and staked it on Curve Finance. Over six months, they earned $800 in rewards—enough to upgrade their espresso machine. Bonus? Their customers now enjoy top-notch lattes while the bakery enjoys a new revenue stream.

Liquidity Pools: Be the Bank

Liquidity pools power decentralized exchanges (DEXs) by allowing users to trade cryptocurrencies seamlessly. In return for providing liquidity, you earn a share of the transaction fees.

- **Example:**
  A user provides $5,000 worth of ETH and USDC to a Uniswap liquidity pool. Each time someone trades ETH for USDC, the user earns a fee. It's like owning a toll booth on the blockchain highway.

Case Study: The Brewery That Built a Liquidity Pool

A craft brewery in Denver decided to experiment with a liquidity pool for their tokenized loyalty program. By creating a trading pair (BeerToken/USDC) on Uniswap, they not only engaged crypto-savvy customers but also earned $2,000 in fees over three months.

Risk Management for DeFi Enthusiasts

High returns often come with high risks, so approach DeFi with a mix of enthusiasm and caution.

- **Smart Contract Risks:** Choose audited platforms with a proven track record (e.g., Aave, Uniswap).
- **Impermanent Loss:** Understand this phenomenon, where price changes can reduce your returns in liquidity pools.
- **Diversify:** Don't put all your assets into one protocol—spread across multiple platforms and blockchains.

Pro Tip: Use insurance services like Nexus Mutual to protect your DeFi investments against potential losses.

Financial Crisis Readiness

When the market looks like a bad rollercoaster, you need strategies to stay afloat.

Stablecoins: The Calm in the Storm

Stablecoins (like USDC, USDT, or DAI) are pegged to traditional assets like the U.S. dollar, offering a "crypto cash" option that doesn't swing wildly in value.

- **How to Use Stablecoins:**
    1. Shift volatile holdings into stablecoins during market downturns.
    2. Use them to pay suppliers, employees, or expenses while avoiding conversion fees.
    3. Earn interest by staking stablecoins on DeFi platforms.

Case Study: The Fashion Startup's Survival Strategy

A fashion brand in Los Angeles relied on crypto sales for 40% of their revenue. When Bitcoin dropped 30% in a week, they converted their reserves into USDC to stabilize operations. Not only did they avoid losses, but they also earned 5% APY on their holdings through BlockFi. Crisis averted, and cash flow secured.

Advanced Crypto Tools for Success

Equip yourself with these tools to execute advanced strategies like a pro:

1. **Zapper.fi**: Simplifies DeFi portfolio management across multiple platforms.
2. **Ledger Live**: Securely manage crypto assets with a hardware wallet.
3. **DeFi Saver**: Automate complex strategies like debt refinancing or liquidation protection.
4. **Nexus Mutual**: Provides insurance against smart contract failures.

Final Takeaway

Advanced crypto strategies require a mix of knowledge, discipline, and the right tools. By mastering behavioral finance, diving into DeFi opportunities, and preparing for market volatility, you'll be ready to navigate the crypto frontier with confidence—and maybe even a little swagger.

Chapter 15: Expanding Horizons: Global and Sustainable Trends

Global Perspectives on Crypto

Cryptocurrency is a global phenomenon, with each region adding its own flavor to the mix. From Africa's innovative mobile payments to Asia's blockchain-driven supply chains, the crypto revolution is as diverse as it is impactful.

Regional Highlights

1. **El Salvador: Bitcoin Nation**
   In 2021, El Salvador became the first country to make Bitcoin legal tender. The government introduced the Chivo Wallet, and businesses across the country were required to accept Bitcoin.

   Case Study:
   A family-owned restaurant in San Salvador saw a 40% increase in revenue after accepting Bitcoin, thanks to crypto tourism. International travelers, excited to spend Bitcoin, flocked to the eatery, turning it into a viral sensation on social media.

2. **Nigeria: Crypto for Everyday Life**
   With high inflation and currency instability, Nigerians have turned to cryptocurrency for remittances and day-to-day transactions. Peer-to-peer trading platforms like Paxful dominate the market.

   Case Study:
   A small retail business in Lagos started accepting Bitcoin for payment. By avoiding traditional banking fees, they cut costs by 15% annually, reinvesting the savings into inventory.

3. **Singapore: Crypto Hub**
   Known for its progressive regulations, Singapore has become a hotspot for blockchain innovation.

   Case Study:
   A fintech startup used Singapore's favorable policies to launch a stablecoin pegged to the Singapore dollar, enabling seamless cross-border payments for Southeast Asian businesses.

Environmental Impact and Sustainability

Cryptocurrency's environmental impact has been a hot topic, but the industry is evolving. With greener technologies like Proof of Stake and renewable energy mining, sustainability is no longer an afterthought.

Making Crypto Mining Sustainable

- **Iceland's Geothermal Mining:**
  Crypto miners in Iceland tap into the country's abundant geothermal energy, proving that mining can be both efficient and eco-friendly.

Case Study:
A blockchain startup partnered with Icelandic miners to ensure their token was sustainably produced, gaining investor trust and a 20% premium on token sales.

- **Ethereum's Transition to Proof of Stake:**
In 2022, Ethereum switched from Proof of Work to Proof of Stake, reducing energy consumption by 99.95%.

Pro Tip: When choosing cryptocurrencies to hold or use, prioritize projects that focus on sustainability.

Crypto and E-Commerce

The intersection of e-commerce and crypto is where digital meets dollars—or Bitcoin, for that matter. Accepting crypto payments not only reduces fees but also opens your store to a global audience.

How to Implement Crypto Payments

1. **Choose a Payment Processor**:
   - **BitPay**: Reliable and integrates easily with major platforms like Shopify.
   - **Coinbase Commerce**: Ideal for businesses needing automatic fiat conversion.
2. **Advertise Your Crypto-Friendliness**: A simple "We Accept Crypto" badge can attract tech-savvy customers.

Case Study: The Sneaker Success Story

A premium sneaker retailer in New York began accepting Ethereum and saw a 20% increase in international sales. By offering automatic fiat conversion, they avoided volatility risks and saved $5,000 in transaction fees over a year.

Final Takeaway

From global adoption to sustainable mining and seamless e-commerce integration, crypto is shaping industries worldwide. Businesses that embrace these trends will not only survive but thrive in this evolving landscape.

Chapter 16: Future-Proofing Your Business: Legal and Compliance Essentials

"If you think compliance is expensive, try non-compliance." – Former Regulator, Probably

When it comes to cryptocurrency, the stakes are high—not just in market volatility but in the regulatory landscape. Governments around the world are cracking down on illicit activities, and businesses must navigate the maze of **KYC (Know Your Customer)** and **AML (Anti-Money Laundering)** rules to stay compliant. The good news? With a little preparation, you can turn compliance into a competitive advantage.

Why KYC/AML Compliance Matters

Crypto's promise of decentralization and anonymity has made it a breeding ground for innovation—and for financial crime. Regulators require businesses to know their customers and monitor transactions to prevent fraud, money laundering, and other illegal activities. Failure to comply can result in severe penalties, from hefty fines to criminal charges.

Key Concepts

- **KYC (Know Your Customer):**
  The process of verifying the identity of your customers to ensure they are who they claim to be. Think of it as a digital

handshake that confirms you're dealing with legitimate individuals or entities.

- **AML (Anti-Money Laundering):**
  A broader framework for detecting and preventing criminal activities like money laundering, terrorism financing, and tax evasion. It goes beyond customer verification to include transaction monitoring and reporting suspicious activity.

What Happens If You Don't Comply?

- In 2020, a European crypto exchange was fined $1.5 million for failing to implement KYC procedures.
- A fintech startup lost its banking partner after neglecting AML reporting, forcing them to shut down operations.

Steps to Ensure Compliance

Compliance doesn't have to be overwhelming. With the right systems and strategies, you can protect your business while maintaining smooth operations.

1. Implement a Robust KYC Process

Think of KYC as your front-line defense. It's about verifying your customer's identity before onboarding them.

How to Do It:

- Collect government-issued IDs, proof of address, and relevant business documentation for corporate clients.
- Use automated tools like **Jumio** or **Onfido** to streamline the verification process.
- Store customer data securely to comply with data protection laws like GDPR.

Case Study:
A U.S.-based crypto exchange adopted an automated KYC system, reducing onboarding time by 40% while flagging high-risk accounts. The result? Faster growth and increased trust from regulators and users.

---

2. Monitor Transactions in Real-Time

AML compliance doesn't stop at onboarding. You need to keep an eye on transactions to identify suspicious patterns.

How to Do It:

- Use blockchain analytics tools like **Chainalysis** or **Elliptic** to detect unusual activity.
- Set thresholds for high-risk transactions (e.g., anything above $10,000) and require additional verification for such cases.
- Train employees to recognize red flags, such as unusually structured payments or frequent small transfers.

Case Study:
A DeFi platform implemented Chainalysis for transaction monitoring and detected a bot funneling illicit funds. By reporting the activity, they avoided regulatory scrutiny and gained credibility in the market.

---

3. File Suspicious Activity Reports (SARs)

If you suspect illegal activity, filing a SAR is often mandatory. This keeps your business compliant and demonstrates proactive risk management.

How to Do It:

- Develop internal policies for identifying when to file a SAR.

- Submit reports promptly to the appropriate financial authority (e.g., FinCEN in the U.S.).
- Maintain records of all SAR filings for future audits.

Case Study:
A fintech company in Europe discovered unusual fund flows through their platform. By filing a timely SAR, they avoided a €500,000 fine and maintained their operating license.

---

4. Stay Updated on Global Regulations

Crypto regulations vary widely across countries, and staying informed is critical for businesses operating internationally.

Examples of Regulatory Environments:

- **Crypto-Friendly:**
    - **Singapore:** Encourages blockchain innovation with clear guidelines.
    - **Switzerland:** Home to "Crypto Valley" and low regulatory hurdles.
- **Restrictive:**
    - **China:** A near-total ban on cryptocurrency trading.
    - **India:** Heavily scrutinizes crypto with ambiguous laws.

Pro Tip:
Work with legal experts to ensure compliance in every region where you operate. Platforms like **LexisNexis Risk Solutions** offer insights into international compliance requirements.

Tools to Simplify KYC/AML Compliance

- **Chainalysis:** Transaction monitoring and blockchain analytics.

- **Jumio/Onfido:** Automated customer verification tools for KYC.
- **CryptoTaxCalculator:** Simplifies recordkeeping for tax and compliance.
- **Nexus Mutual:** Provides insurance for smart contract risks.

Turning Compliance into a Competitive Advantage

While compliance might feel like a chore, it's also an opportunity to differentiate your business. Customers, investors, and regulators are more likely to trust a company that prioritizes security and transparency. By implementing robust KYC/AML measures, you can protect your reputation, avoid penalties, and position yourself as a leader in the crypto space.

Case Study: A Compliance Success Story

A U.K.-based payment platform partnered with Chainalysis to automate compliance procedures. Not only did they reduce operational costs by 30%, but they also attracted a new wave of institutional clients, boosting revenue by 50% within a year.

Final Takeaway

KYC/AML compliance isn't just a box to check—it's a cornerstone for building trust, protecting your reputation, and ensuring your business thrives well into the future. With the right tools, processes, and mindset, you can turn regulatory hurdles into stepping stones for success in the digital economy.

Tax Reporting: What You Need to Know

Crypto transactions are no longer under the radar. The IRS is serious about digital asset reporting, as evidenced by a clear statement on the 1040 tax return for 2023:

"At any time during 202X, did you: (a) receive (as a reward, award, or payment for property or services); or (b) sell, exchange, or otherwise dispose of a digital asset (or a financial interest in a digital asset)?"

By checking "yes or no," you affirm under penalty of perjury that your reporting is accurate. If your CPA isn't asking you about your crypto activity, it might be time to reconsider your advisor.

Pro Tip:
A CPA familiar with cryptocurrency can help you:

- Track your transactions accurately.
- Report gains or losses on Form 8949 and Schedule D.
- Avoid penalties by adhering to the latest IRS guidelines.

We Can Help: If your CPA isn't up to speed, consider working with professionals who understand both digital assets and tax compliance. We've got the expertise to make sure you're covered.

Conclusion

Congratulations—you've made it to the end of this wild, wonderful journey through crypto, cash flow, and financial freedom. You're officially part of **the elite 1%** who don't just daydream about a better financial future but actually do something about it. While the rest of the world is binge-watching cat videos and arguing about pineapple on pizza, you've been laying the groundwork for a life of digital dominance and financial independence. Bravo!

The strategies in this book—especially the gems hidden in this bonus section—aren't just tips; they're your cheat codes to navigating the ever-evolving game of money. Crypto isn't just the future; it's happening now. Cash flow isn't just a business term; it's your financial heartbeat. And financial freedom? That's not just the end goal—it's the reward for embracing the journey.

Here's the deal: the digital economy rewards the bold, the informed, and the persistent. Keep learning, experimenting, and making smart (and occasionally gutsy) moves. Whether it's buying your first NFT, setting up a crypto wallet, or finally getting that cash flow under control, every step forward matters.

The future is yours to shape—so go out there and make it one worth living. Oh, and if anyone asks how you became such a financial wizard, feel free to tell them about this book. Or just wink mysteriously and say, "I know a guy." Either way, the world is waiting for your next move. Let's see what you've got!

Glossary of Terms (Because Jargon Doesn't Have to Be Boring)

Crypto and Blockchain Terms

Altcoin: Any cryptocurrency that isn't Bitcoin. Think of them as the indie bands of the crypto world—sometimes groundbreaking, sometimes just a guy with a ukulele.

Blockchain: A digital ledger that keeps track of transactions. Imagine a magical notebook that everyone owns a copy of, where no one can sneak in and erase what they owe you.

Bitcoin: The Beyoncé of the crypto world. It's the one everyone knows, talks about, and wants a piece of.

Cold Wallet: A cryptocurrency wallet not connected to the internet. It's like hiding your cash in a safe, except the safe is made of ones and zeros and can fit in your pocket.

Crypto Mining: The process of validating cryptocurrency transactions and adding them to the blockchain. Think of it as digital gold mining—minus the pickaxes and canaries.

Decentralization: Like a party where no one's in charge, but somehow, the music's still playing, and the snacks haven't run out. That's the magic of decentralization.

Decentralized Finance (DeFi): The Wild West of finance, where you can lend, borrow, and trade crypto without a bank breathing down your neck.

It's freedom... with a side of volatility.

Ethereum: The Swiss Army knife of crypto. It's not just money; it's a platform for building apps, smart contracts, and all sorts of decentralized shenanigans.

Gas Fees: The price you pay to get your Ethereum transactions moving. Think of it as the toll you pay on the blockchain highway.

HODL: A typo-turned-mantra for crypto enthusiasts, meaning "Hold On for Dear Life." It's what you do when your Bitcoin drops 30% overnight.

Hot Wallet: A cryptocurrency wallet connected to the internet for easy access. Convenient, yes. Secure? About as secure as leaving your front door unlocked.

Impermanent Loss: The temporary loss of value when providing liquidity to a DeFi pool due to price fluctuations of the paired tokens. It's like watching your favorite sweater stretch out in the wash—painful, but fixable.

Layer-2 Scaling Solution: Technologies built on top of blockchains to speed up transactions and reduce fees. Think of them as the fast lanes on a congested highway—fewer tolls, faster rides.

Liquidity: Your ability to turn assets into cash faster than you can say "unexpected expense." It's the difference between having a Picasso painting and having dollar bills.

Liquidity Pool: A stash of crypto assets locked in a smart contract to enable trading on decentralized exchanges. It's like the community tip jar for crypto trading—everyone chips in to keep things moving.

Market Capitalization: The total value of all the coins in circulation. It's like weighing the entire crypto pie to see how big it is.

Meme Coin: A cryptocurrency that started as a joke but somehow gained value (looking at you, Dogecoin). It's the financial world's version of a viral TikTok video.

Mining: The process of validating transactions on a blockchain and earning rewards. Picture it as a digital treasure hunt, but instead of shovels, miners use computers.

NFT (Non-Fungible Token): A unique digital asset that proves you own something. It's like having a digital birth certificate for your Bored Ape or that one pixel you bought for a million dollars.

Private Key: The secret password to your crypto wallet. Lose this, and you'll wish you could cryogenically freeze yourself until someone invents quantum crypto recovery.

Rug Pull: A crypto scam where developers abandon a project and run off with investors' funds. It's like buying a car, only to discover the seller took the wheels and engine.

Satoshi Nakamoto: The Banksy of the crypto world. No one knows who they are, but they left us a masterpiece: Bitcoin.

Smart Contract:
A digital agreement that executes itself when conditions are met. It's like a vending machine: insert coin, get snack—only with less chance of it eating your money.

Stablecoin:
A cryptocurrency tied to a stable asset like the U.S. dollar. Think of it as the designated driver of the crypto party—it keeps things grounded.

Whale: Someone who holds a massive amount of cryptocurrency. They can make waves in the market just by buying or selling.

Volatility: The wild price swings in cryptocurrency. One day your portfolio is buying you a yacht, the next day it's buying you a burger (but not the fries).

Business and Financial Terms

Accounts Receivable (AR): The money your customers owe you but haven't paid yet. It's like lending your friend $20 and hoping they remember before your next coffee run.

Asset Class: A group of investments that behave similarly in the market. Examples include stocks, bonds, and now, cryptocurrencies. Bitcoin and Ethereum are like the "cool kids" of the crypto asset class.

Cash Flow: The movement of cash in and out of your business. Positive cash flow is like a full gas tank—you can keep going. Negative cash flow? That's a sputtering engine.

Expense Audit: A no-nonsense review of where your money's going. Spoiler alert: you'll probably find some "necessary" costs, like that premium coffee subscription no one remembers signing up for.

Financial Freedom: When your money works for you instead of the other way around. It's what happens when you're not sweating over the electric bill while sipping cocktails on a Tuesday.

KYC (Know Your Customer): A process where platforms verify your identity to comply with regulations. It's like showing your ID at a bar, but instead of tequila, you're getting access to crypto services.

Liquidity: The ability to pay your bills when they're due. If your bank balance is as dry as your grandma's Thanksgiving turkey, you're in trouble.

Net Profit: The money left after all your expenses are paid. It's the financial equivalent of finishing your plate and still having dessert waiting.

Profit Margin: The percentage of revenue that becomes profit. The higher, the better—it's like the cherry on top of your financial sundae.

ROI (Return on Investment): How much you gain from your investments, expressed as a percentage. If it's negative, maybe investing in that alpaca farm wasn't such a great idea.

Scalability: The ability of your business to grow without breaking the bank. It's like upgrading from a tricycle to a sports car, but the gas mileage stays the same.

Working Capital: The cash available to cover daily operations. It's your financial fuel, keeping the business engine running smoothly.

References

Books

1. *Mastering Bitcoin* by Andreas M. Antonopoulos
   A comprehensive guide to Bitcoin, blockchain technology, and cryptocurrency fundamentals.
2. *The Bitcoin Standard* by Saifedean Ammous
   Explains Bitcoin's role as "sound money" and its potential to disrupt traditional finance.
3. *Blockchain Basics* by Daniel Drescher
   Ideal for beginners, this book breaks down blockchain concepts into easy-to-understand explanations.
4. *Cryptoassets: The Innovative Investor's Guide to Bitcoin and Beyond* by Chris Burniske and Jack Tatar
   Focuses on evaluating and investing in cryptocurrencies and blockchain projects.
5. *DeFi and the Future of Finance* by Campbell R. Harvey
   Explores decentralized finance and how it is revolutionizing the financial industry.

Articles

1. *"The Basics of Bitcoins and Blockchains"* (Investopedia) Covers fundamental concepts like mining, wallets, and blockchain.
2. *"A Beginner's Guide to Cryptocurrency"* (CoinDesk) Provides a broad introduction to cryptocurrency, from buying your first coin to understanding market trends.
3. *"How Blockchain Technology Works"* (MIT Technology Review)
   A high-level overview of blockchain technology and its applications.
4. *"Stablecoins: What They Are and Why They Matter"* (CoinTelegraph)
   Explores the growing role of stablecoins in the crypto ecosystem.
5. *"The Role of Stablecoins in Business Transactions"* (CoinTelegraph)
   Discusses how businesses are stabilizing cash flow with stablecoins.
   Link: https://cointelegraph.com
6. *"Blockchain Beyond Crypto: Tools for Managing Modern Businesses"* (MIT Technology Review) Highlights blockchain applications in business, including cash flow management.
7. *"How Businesses Leverage Bitcoin for International Payments"* (Forbes, 2024)
   Explores how firms optimize cash flow using Bitcoin for cross-border transactions.

Tools

1. **Coinbase Commerce**
   Accept crypto payments seamlessly, with options to convert funds to fiat.
   Link: https://commerce.coinbase.com
2. **BitPay**
   A robust payment platform enabling crypto acceptance with conversion features.
   Link: https://bitpay.com

3. **CoinTracker**
   Simplifies crypto portfolio tracking and tax calculations.
   Link: https://www.cointracker.io
4. **QuickBooks (Crypto Integrations)**
   Integrates traditional accounting with crypto tracking tools.
   Link: https://quickbooks.intuit.com
5. **DeFi Pulse**
   Tracks decentralized finance projects, ideal for monitoring liquidity solutions.
   Link: https://defipulse.com
6. **Float**
   A forecasting tool for creating accurate cash flow projections.
   Link: https://floatapp.com
7. **CryptoTaxCalculator**
   Calculates the tax implications of crypto transactions in business.
   Link: https://cryptotaxcalculator.io
8. **Trezor and Ledger Wallets**
   Secure hardware wallets for protecting long-term crypto reserves offline.
   Link: https://trezor.io | https://www.ledger.com

Case Studies

1. *"How Businesses Leverage Bitcoin for International Payments"* (Forbes, 2024)
   Explores how firms optimize cash flow using Bitcoin for cross-border transactions.
   Link: https://www.forbes.com
2. *"Crypto Success Stories: Real-World Applications of Digital Currencies in Business"* (CoinDesk, 2024)
   Highlights businesses integrating crypto into daily operations.
   Link: https://www.coindesk.com
3. *"The Impact of Blockchain on Supply Chain Management"* (Harvard Business Review, 2024)
   Discusses blockchain's role in improving transparency and efficiency.
   Link: https://hbr.org

Additional Academic References

1. **Catalini, C., & Tucker, C. (2017).** *The digital privacy paradox: Small money, small costs, small talk.* National Bureau of Economic Research.
2. **Schoar, A., & Makarov, I. (2021).** *Bitcoin: Who owns it, who mines it, who's breaking the law.* MIT Sloan.
3. **Catalini, C. (2017).** *How blockchain technology will impact the digital economy.* Oxford Business Law Blog.

Appendix A: Satoshi Nakamoto's White Paper Summary

Bitcoin: A Peer-to-Peer Electronic Cash System

Satoshi Nakamoto
satoshin@gmx.com
www.bitcoin.org

Abstract. A purely peer-to-peer version of electronic cash would allow online payments to be sent directly from one party to another without going through a financial institution. Digital signatures provide part of the solution, but the main benefits are lost if a trusted third party is still required to prevent double-spending. We propose a solution to the double-spending problem using a peer-to-peer network. The network timestamps transactions by hashing them into an ongoing chain of hash-based proof-of-work, forming a record that cannot be changed without redoing the proof-of-work. The longest chain not only serves as proof of the sequence of events witnessed, but proof that it came from the largest pool of CPU power. As long as a majority of CPU power is controlled by nodes that are not cooperating to attack the network, they'll generate the longest chain and outpace attackers. The network itself requires minimal structure. Messages are broadcast on a best effort basis, and nodes can leave and rejoin the network at will, accepting the longest proof-of-work chain as proof of what happened while they were gone.

1. Introduction

Commerce on the Internet has come to rely almost exclusively on financial institutions serving as trusted third parties to process electronic payments. While the system works well enough for most transactions, it still suffers from the inherent weaknesses of the trust based model. Completely non-reversible transactions are not really possible, since financial institutions cannot avoid mediating disputes. The cost of mediation increases transaction costs, limiting the minimum practical transaction size and cutting off the possibility for small casual transactions, and there is a broader cost in the loss of ability to make non-reversible payments for non-reversible services. With the possibility of reversal, the need for trust spreads. Merchants must be wary of their customers, hassling them for more information than they would otherwise need. A certain percentage of fraud is accepted as unavoidable. These costs and payment uncertainties can be avoided in person by using physical currency, but no mechanism exists to make payments over a communications channel without a trusted party.

What is needed is an electronic payment system based on cryptographic proof instead of trust, allowing any two willing parties to transact directly with each other without the need for a trusted third party. Transactions that are computationally impractical to reverse would protect sellers from fraud, and routine escrow mechanisms could easily be implemented to protect buyers. In this paper, we propose a solution to the double-spending problem using a peer-to-peer distributed timestamp server to generate computational proof of the chronological order of transactions. The system is secure as long as honest nodes collectively control more CPU power than any cooperating group of attacker nodes.

2. Transactions

We define an electronic coin as a chain of digital signatures. Each owner transfers the coin to the next by digitally signing a hash of the previous transaction and the public key of the next owner and adding these to the end of the coin. A payee can verify the signatures to verify the chain of ownership.

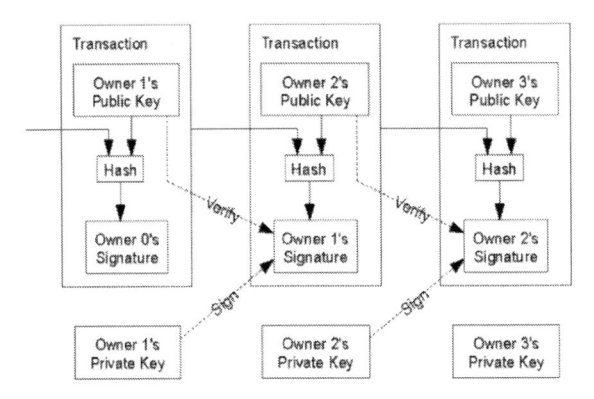

The problem of course is the payee can't verify that one of the owners did not double-spend the coin. A common solution is to introduce a trusted central authority, or mint, that checks every transaction for double spending. After each transaction, the coin must be returned to the mint to issue a new coin, and only coins issued directly from the mint are trusted not to be double-spent. The problem with this solution is that the fate of the entire money system depends on the company running the mint, with every transaction having to go through them, just like a bank.

We need a way for the payee to know that the previous owners did not sign any earlier transactions. For our purposes, the earliest transaction is the one that counts, so we don't care about later attempts to double-spend. The only way to confirm the absence of a transaction is to be aware of all transactions. In the mint based model, the mint was aware of all transactions and decided which arrived first. To accomplish this without a trusted party, transactions must be publicly announced [1], and we need a system for participants to agree on a single history of the order in which they were received. The payee needs proof that at the time of each transaction, the majority of nodes agreed it was the first received.

3. Timestamp Server

The solution we propose begins with a timestamp server. A timestamp server works by taking a hash of a block of items to be timestamped and widely publishing the hash, such as in a newspaper or Usenet post [2-5]. The timestamp proves that the data must have existed at the time, obviously, in order to get into the hash. Each timestamp includes the previous timestamp in its hash, forming a chain, with each additional timestamp reinforcing the ones before it.

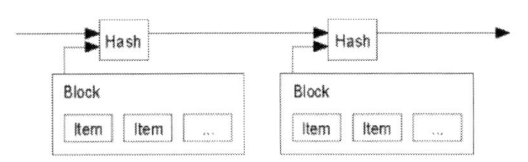

4. Proof-of-Work

To implement a distributed timestamp server on a peer-to-peer basis, we will need to use a proof-of-work system similar to Adam Back's Hashcash [6], rather than newspaper or Usenet posts. The proof-of-work involves scanning for a value that when hashed, such as with SHA-256, the hash begins with a number of zero bits. The average work required is exponential in the number of zero bits required and can be verified by executing a single hash.

For our timestamp network, we implement the proof-of-work by incrementing a nonce in the block until a value is found that gives the block's hash the required zero bits. Once the CPU effort has been expended to make it satisfy the proof-of-work, the block cannot be changed without redoing the work. As later blocks are chained after it, the work to change the block would include redoing all the blocks after it.

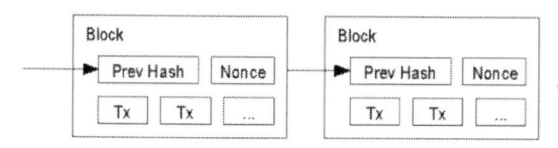

The proof-of-work also solves the problem of determining representation in majority decision making. If the majority were based on one-IP-address-one-vote, it could be subverted by anyone able to allocate many IPs. Proof-of-work is essentially one-CPU-one-vote. The majority decision is represented by the longest chain, which has the greatest proof-of-work effort invested in it. If a majority of CPU power is controlled by honest nodes, the honest chain will grow the fastest and outpace any competing chains. To modify a past block, an attacker would have to redo the proof-of-work of the block and all blocks after it and then catch up with and surpass the work of the honest nodes. We will show later that the probability of a slower attacker catching up diminishes exponentially as subsequent blocks are added.

To compensate for increasing hardware speed and varying interest in running nodes over time, the proof-of-work difficulty is determined by a moving average targeting an average number of blocks per hour. If they're generated too fast, the difficulty increases.

5. Network

The steps to run the network are as follows:

1) New transactions are broadcast to all nodes.
2) Each node collects new transactions into a block.
3) Each node works on finding a difficult proof-of-work for its block.
4) When a node finds a proof-of-work, it broadcasts the block to all nodes.
5) Nodes accept the block only if all transactions in it are valid and not already spent.
6) Nodes express their acceptance of the block by working on creating the next block in the chain, using the hash of the accepted block as the previous hash.

Nodes always consider the longest chain to be the correct one and will keep working on extending it. If two nodes broadcast different versions of the next block simultaneously, some nodes may receive one or the other first. In that case, they work on the first one they received, but save the other branch in case it becomes longer. The tie will be broken when the next proof-of-work is found and one branch becomes longer; the nodes that were working on the other branch will then switch to the longer one.

New transaction broadcasts do not necessarily need to reach all nodes. As long as they reach many nodes, they will get into a block before long. Block broadcasts are also tolerant of dropped messages. If a node does not receive a block, it will request it when it receives the next block and realizes it missed one.

6. Incentive

By convention, the first transaction in a block is a special transaction that starts a new coin owned by the creator of the block. This adds an incentive for nodes to support the network, and provides a way to initially distribute coins into circulation, since there is no central authority to issue them. The steady addition of a constant of amount of new coins is analogous to gold miners expending resources to add gold to circulation. In our case, it is CPU time and electricity that is expended.

The incentive can also be funded with transaction fees. If the output value of a transaction is less than its input value, the difference is a transaction fee that is added to the incentive value of the block containing the transaction. Once a predetermined number of coins have entered circulation, the incentive can transition entirely to transaction fees and be completely inflation free.

The incentive may help encourage nodes to stay honest. If a greedy attacker is able to assemble more CPU power than all the honest nodes, he would have to choose between using it to defraud people by stealing back his payments, or using it to generate new coins. He ought to find it more profitable to play by the rules, such rules that favour him with more new coins than everyone else combined, than to undermine the system and the validity of his own wealth.

7. Reclaiming Disk Space

Once the latest transaction in a coin is buried under enough blocks, the spent transactions before it can be discarded to save disk space. To facilitate this without breaking the block's hash, transactions are hashed in a Merkle Tree [7][2][5], with only the root included in the block's hash. Old blocks can then be compacted by stubbing off branches of the tree. The interior hashes do not need to be stored.

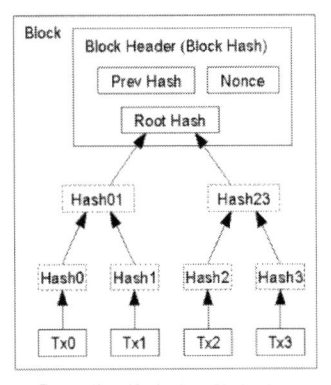

Transactions Hashed in a Merkle Tree 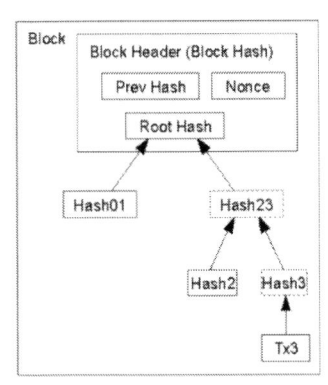   After Pruning Tx0-2 from the Block

A block header with no transactions would be about 80 bytes. If we suppose blocks are generated every 10 minutes, 80 bytes * 6 * 24 * 365 = 4.2MB per year. With computer systems typically selling with 2GB of RAM as of 2008, and Moore's Law predicting current growth of 1.2GB per year, storage should not be a problem even if the block headers must be kept in memory.

8. Simplified Payment Verification

It is possible to verify payments without running a full network node. A user only needs to keep a copy of the block headers of the longest proof-of-work chain, which he can get by querying network nodes until he's convinced he has the longest chain, and obtain the Merkle branch linking the transaction to the block it's timestamped in. He can't check the transaction for himself, but by linking it to a place in the chain, he can see that a network node has accepted it, and blocks added after it further confirm the network has accepted it.

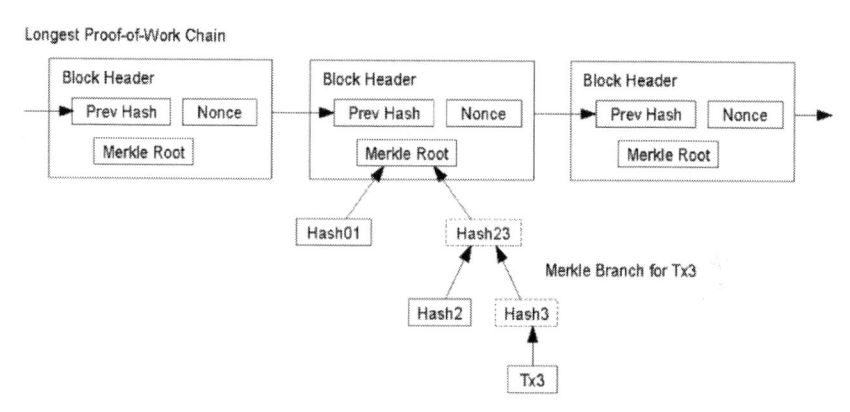

As such, the verification is reliable as long as honest nodes control the network, but is more vulnerable if the network is overpowered by an attacker. While network nodes can verify transactions for themselves, the simplified method can be fooled by an attacker's fabricated transactions for as long as the attacker can continue to overpower the network. One strategy to protect against this would be to accept alerts from network nodes when they detect an invalid block, prompting the user's software to download the full block and alerted transactions to confirm the inconsistency. Businesses that receive frequent payments will probably still want to run their own nodes for more independent security and quicker verification.

9. Combining and Splitting Value

Although it would be possible to handle coins individually, it would be unwieldy to make a separate transaction for every cent in a transfer. To allow value to be split and combined, transactions contain multiple inputs and outputs. Normally there will be either a single input from a larger previous transaction or multiple inputs combining smaller amounts, and at most two outputs: one for the payment, and one returning the change, if any, back to the sender.

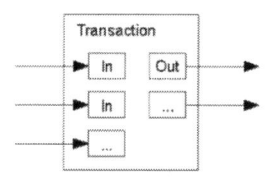

It should be noted that fan-out, where a transaction depends on several transactions, and those transactions depend on many more, is not a problem here. There is never the need to extract a complete standalone copy of a transaction's history.

10. Privacy

The traditional banking model achieves a level of privacy by limiting access to information to the parties involved and the trusted third party. The necessity to announce all transactions publicly precludes this method, but privacy can still be maintained by breaking the flow of information in another place: by keeping public keys anonymous. The public can see that someone is sending an amount to someone else, but without information linking the transaction to anyone. This is similar to the level of information released by stock exchanges, where the time and size of individual trades, the "tape", is made public, but without telling who the parties were.

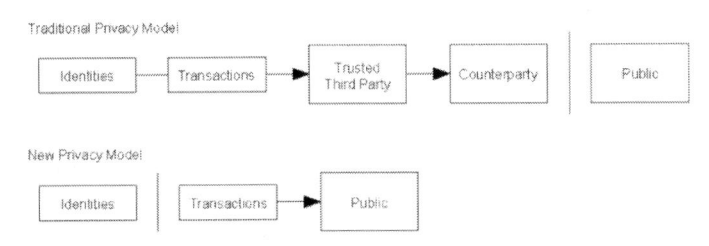

Traditional Privacy Model

Identities → Transactions → Trusted Third Party → Counterparty | Public

New Privacy Model

Identities | Transactions → Public

As an additional firewall, a new key pair should be used for each transaction to keep them from being linked to a common owner. Some linking is still unavoidable with multi-input transactions, which necessarily reveal that their inputs were owned by the same owner. The risk is that if the owner of a key is revealed, linking could reveal other transactions that belonged to the same owner.

11. Calculations

We consider the scenario of an attacker trying to generate an alternate chain faster than the honest chain. Even if this is accomplished, it does not throw the system open to arbitrary changes, such as creating value out of thin air or taking money that never belonged to the attacker. Nodes are not going to accept an invalid transaction as payment, and honest nodes will never accept a block containing them. An attacker can only try to change one of his own transactions to take back money he recently spent.

The race between the honest chain and an attacker chain can be characterized as a Binomial Random Walk. The success event is the honest chain being extended by one block, increasing its lead by +1, and the failure event is the attacker's chain being extended by one block, reducing the gap by -1.

The probability of an attacker catching up from a given deficit is analogous to a Gambler's Ruin problem. Suppose a gambler with unlimited credit starts at a deficit and plays potentially an infinite number of trials to try to reach breakeven. We can calculate the probability he ever reaches breakeven, or that an attacker ever catches up with the honest chain, as follows [8]:

p = probability an honest node finds the next block
q = probability the attacker finds the next block
q_z = probability the attacker will ever catch up from z blocks behind

$$q_z = \begin{cases} 1 & \text{if } p \leq q \\ (q/p)^z & \text{if } p > q \end{cases}$$

Given our assumption that $p > q$, the probability drops exponentially as the number of blocks the attacker has to catch up with increases. With the odds against him, if he doesn't make a lucky lunge forward early on, his chances become vanishingly small as he falls further behind.

We now consider how long the recipient of a new transaction needs to wait before being sufficiently certain the sender can't change the transaction. We assume the sender is an attacker who wants to make the recipient believe he paid him for a while, then switch it to pay back to himself after some time has passed. The receiver will be alerted when that happens, but the sender hopes it will be too late.

The receiver generates a new key pair and gives the public key to the sender shortly before signing. This prevents the sender from preparing a chain of blocks ahead of time by working on it continuously until he is lucky enough to get far enough ahead, then executing the transaction at that moment. Once the transaction is sent, the dishonest sender starts working in secret on a parallel chain containing an alternate version of his transaction.

The recipient waits until the transaction has been added to a block and z blocks have been linked after it. He doesn't know the exact amount of progress the attacker has made, but assuming the honest blocks took the average expected time per block, the attacker's potential progress will be a Poisson distribution with expected value:

$$\lambda = z \frac{q}{p}$$

To get the probability the attacker could still catch up now, we multiply the Poisson density for each amount of progress he could have made by the probability he could catch up from that point:

$$\sum_{k=0}^{\infty} \frac{\lambda^k e^{-\lambda}}{k!} \cdot \begin{cases} (q/p)^{(z-k)} & \text{if } k \leq z \\ 1 & \text{if } k > z \end{cases}$$

Rearranging to avoid summing the infinite tail of the distribution...

$$1 - \sum_{k=0}^{z} \frac{\lambda^k e^{-\lambda}}{k!} \left(1 - (q/p)^{(z-k)}\right)$$

Converting to C code...

```c
#include <math.h>
double AttackerSuccessProbability(double q, int z)
{
    double p = 1.0 - q;
    double lambda = z * (q / p);
    double sum = 1.0;
    int i, k;
    for (k = 0; k <= z; k++)
    {
        double poisson = exp(-lambda);
        for (i = 1; i <= k; i++)
            poisson *= lambda / i;
        sum -= poisson * (1 - pow(q / p, z - k));
    }
    return sum;
}
```

Running some results, we can see the probability drop off exponentially with z.

```
q=0.1
z=0     P=1.0000000
z=1     P=0.2045873
z=2     P=0.0509779
z=3     P=0.0131722
z=4     P=0.0034552
z=5     P=0.0009137
z=6     P=0.0002428
z=7     P=0.0000647
z=8     P=0.0000173
z=9     P=0.0000046
z=10    P=0.0000012

q=0.3
z=0     P=1.0000000
z=5     P=0.1773523
z=10    P=0.0416605
z=15    P=0.0101008
z=20    P=0.0024804
z=25    P=0.0006132
z=30    P=0.0001522
z=35    P=0.0000379
z=40    P=0.0000095
z=45    P=0.0000024
z=50    P=0.0000006
```

Solving for P less than 0.1%...

```
P < 0.001
q=0.10    z=5
q=0.15    z=8
q=0.20    z=11
q=0.25    z=15
q=0.30    z=24
q=0.35    z=41
q=0.40    z=89
q=0.45    z=340
```

12. Conclusion

We have proposed a system for electronic transactions without relying on trust. We started with the usual framework of coins made from digital signatures, which provides strong control of ownership, but is incomplete without a way to prevent double-spending. To solve this, we proposed a peer-to-peer network using proof-of-work to record a public history of transactions that quickly becomes computationally impractical for an attacker to change if honest nodes control a majority of CPU power. The network is robust in its unstructured simplicity. Nodes work all at once with little coordination. They do not need to be identified, since messages are not routed to any particular place and only need to be delivered on a best effort basis. Nodes can leave and rejoin the network at will, accepting the proof-of-work chain as proof of what happened while they were gone. They vote with their CPU power, expressing their acceptance of valid blocks by working on extending them and rejecting invalid blocks by refusing to work on them. Any needed rules and incentives can be enforced with this consensus mechanism.

References

[1] W. Dai, "b-money," http://www.weidai.com/bmoney.txt, 1998.

[2] H. Massias, X.S. Avila, and J.-J. Quisquater, "Design of a secure timestamping service with minimal trust requirements," In *20th Symposium on Information Theory in the Benelux*, May 1999.

[3] S. Haber, W.S. Stornetta, "How to time-stamp a digital document," In *Journal of Cryptology*, vol 3, no 2, pages 99-111, 1991.

[4] D. Bayer, S. Haber, W.S. Stornetta, "Improving the efficiency and reliability of digital time-stamping," In *Sequences II: Methods in Communication, Security and Computer Science*, pages 329-334, 1993.

[5] S. Haber, W.S. Stornetta, "Secure names for bit-strings," In *Proceedings of the 4th ACM Conference on Computer and Communications Security*, pages 28-35, April 1997.

[6] A. Back, "Hashcash - a denial of service counter-measure," http://www.hashcash.org/papers/hashcash.pdf, 2002.

[7] R.C. Merkle, "Protocols for public key cryptosystems," In *Proc. 1980 Symposium on Security and Privacy*, IEEE Computer Society, pages 122-133, April 1980.

[8] W. Feller, "An introduction to probability theory and its applications," 1957.

Appendix B: Example Financial Freedom Roadmap

Financial freedom doesn't happen overnight—it's a journey that requires planning, persistence, and a little strategic thinking. This roadmap provides a practical example for building a freedom-focused financial future, integrating cryptocurrency and cash flow strategies to maximize success.

Phase 1: Define Your Goals (Year 1)

"If you don't know where you're going, any road will take you there." – Lewis Carroll

1. **Clarify Your Vision**
    - Ask yourself: *What does financial freedom mean to me?* Is it early retirement, launching a passion project, or creating generational wealth?
    - Define measurable goals: e.g., "Achieve $1,000,000 in net worth by 2030" or "Build a $10,000/month passive income stream."

2. **Assess Your Current Position**
    - Calculate your net worth: Assets - Liabilities.
    - Track monthly cash flow: Income - Expenses.
    - Identify gaps: Are you overspending? Are your assets underperforming?

3. **Educate Yourself**

- Learn about cryptocurrency basics, cash flow management, and risk mitigation.
- Resources: Books like *The Bitcoin Standard* or tools like CoinDesk for crypto trends.

4. **Start Small with Crypto**
    - Allocate 1-5% of your investment portfolio to major cryptocurrencies (e.g., Bitcoin, Ethereum).
    - Use a secure wallet and avoid speculative trading until you're confident.

Phase 2: Build Momentum (Years 2-3)

"Small daily improvements over time lead to stunning results." – Robin Sharma

1. **Optimize Cash Flow**
    - Implement strategies to accelerate receivables and minimize unnecessary expenses.
    - Build a cash reserve covering at least 3-6 months of operating expenses.

2. **Increase Investments**
    - Gradually increase your exposure to cryptocurrencies, focusing on blue-chip tokens.
    - Diversify with stablecoins and DeFi platforms for lending or earning passive income.

3. **Leverage Technology**
    - Use tools like QuickBooks for tracking finances and Coinbase Commerce for accepting crypto payments.

- Explore yield farming or liquidity pools for higher returns, but stay cautious.

4. **Secure Your Foundation**
   - Pay down high-interest debts.
   - Reinvest profits into scalable assets, such as index funds or business expansion.

Phase 3: Expand and Diversify (Years 4-6)

"Don't put all your eggs in one basket." – Warren Buffett

1. **Expand Investment Portfolios**
   - Venture into altcoins with real-world use cases (e.g., Ethereum, Solana, Cardano).
   - Balance speculative investments with stable, low-volatility assets.

2. **Create Passive Income Streams**
   - Generate revenue through staking, lending, and dividend-paying investments.
   - Explore real-world applications for crypto, such as tokenizing assets or utilizing NFTs.

3. **Invest in Education and Skills**
   - Take courses on advanced financial planning or blockchain technologies.
   - Attend conferences to network with industry leaders and gain new insights.

Phase 4: Achieve Financial Independence (Years 7-10)

"The goal isn't more money. The goal is living life on your terms." – Chris Brogan

1. **Reassess and Refine Goals**
   - Evaluate progress toward initial milestones.
   - Adjust your roadmap to align with any shifts in priorities or market conditions.

2. **Scale Back Active Income**
   - Transition from hands-on work to managing passive investments.
   - Delegate business operations or explore partial ownership models.

3. **Protect Wealth**
   - Establish trusts or funds for legacy planning.
   - Consult financial advisors to minimize tax liabilities.

4. **Live Aligned with Your Values**
   - Use financial freedom to support causes, travel, or pursue personal passions.
   - Celebrate milestones, but remain vigilant against complacency.

Tools to Stay on Track

- **Budgeting Software**: Mint, YNAB, or QuickBooks for cash flow tracking.
- **Investment Platforms**: Coinbase, Binance, or Kraken for crypto; Vanguard for traditional investments.

- **Educational Resources**: Online courses from Coursera, Khan Academy, or your MIT Blockchain Technologies network.
- **Advisors**: Financial planners with expertise in cryptocurrency and blockchain.

Final Note:

Financial freedom isn't just about achieving a specific number—it's about creating options, security, and alignment with your values. Follow this roadmap, adjust as needed, and remember: The journey is just as important as the destination.

ABOUT THE AUTHOR

A passionate cryptocurrency advocate, Chris believes blockchain technology is the future of money—a transformative moment akin to the dawn of the internet. Having worked with countless businesses that see cryptocurrency as an intimidating, foreign concept, Chris is on a mission to make this revolutionary technology accessible and practical. He wrote *Crypto and Cash Flow: A Business Owner's Guide to Financial Freedom* to demystify the crypto space and show entrepreneurs how to harness its potential for financial growth.

Building on the principles in his first book, *The Cash Flow Cure*, Chris emphasizes the importance of financial clarity, profitability, and cash flow as the cornerstones of business success. With a focus on clear, actionable strategies and a knack for making complex topics relatable, Chris empowers his readers to take control of their financial futures with confidence.

Made in the USA
Columbia, SC
04 January 2025